T0154073

PRAISE FOR ANTHONY GERACI AND *EARNING MONEY WHILE YOU SLEEP*

I have known Anthony Geraci for years and thoroughly enjoyed reading his book. Geraci is a non-conventional lending expert and is someone to listen to. The stories he tells and the data he presents clearly demonstrate why private lending is a great investment tool.

— Jeff Levin, Specialty Lending Group

Geraci weaves his personal experiences with outstanding technical knowledge of hard money lending to pull back the curtain on this hidden investment industry. Well worth the read!

— Don Ho, Founder, Harmony Tea Bar

Anthony has clearly accomplished yet another goal he set for himself with this book. He has brought the non-conventional lending industry into those floodlights he mentions in the introduction to his book. He has lead his readers to the water, the question now is, "Will they drink?"

— Josh Nevarez, Partner, Armanino LLP

Anthony weaves both his gripping and amazing personal story with the previously inaccessible nontraditional lending story—leaving the reader spellbound and wiser because of both. Revealing. Surprising. And easily digestible for a marketing guy like me.

—Scott Empringham, CEO and founder, Flashpoint Media

Anthony Geraci has one of the brightest minds in private lending. He also has a very unique vantage point, as he looks at deals not only through the eyes of borrower or lender, but also an attorney. Anthony has built one of the most successful businesses in our space and he brings that knowledge and experience as well as a unique viewpoint in his latest book. You will learn of his ups and downs, and how he has built an amazing law firm with wonderful employees and loyal customers. It is a must read for any real estate investor! You will enjoy this book very much.

— Eddie Wilson, CEO, Affinity Worldwide;
Think Realty; American Association of Private Lenders

Anthony Geraci's life is a an example of perseverance, commitment, and hard work. He kept walking toward his goals at times when most people choose to give up. His life experiences will captivate the reader and his insight from lessons learned in private lending will have a profound impact on lives for generations to come. I highly recommend this book."

—Chad Varga, Author of *Bounce*
The Chad Varga Company

Many years ago we were impressed with Anthony's knowledge, caring, and willingness to help others, and started referring clients to his firm for proper entity structure, licensing, loan documents, investor agreements and many items that must be correct in this increasingly regulated industry. Working together has been wonderful, and helps create the complete, compliant business model needed for all of us to succeed.

—Gordon Albrecht, Senior Director, FCI

It's rare when you find a book from an author with such a unique perspective, and that experience shows in page after page. With humble beginnings to being a major force in the private lending world, Anthony Geraci walks the walk. Anthony Geraci cut his teeth with grunt work at a real estate law firm, and now has an empire. That empire includes having the largest real estate law firm in the country, popular conferences, his own magazine, and years of successful private lending under his belt. The most intriguing aspect of the book is how easy it is to build wealth, with substantial returns and minimum risk, in private lending. Anyone with an IRA or capital to invest should read this book.

—AJ Poulin, The Mortgage Office

EARNING MONEY WHILE YOU SLEEP

ANTHONY GERACI, Esq.

EARNING MONEY

WHILE YOU

SLEEP

ONE SIMPLE SECRET TO
FINANCIAL FREEDOM

Copyright © 2018 by Anthony Geraci.

All rights reserved. No part of this book may be used or reproduced in any manner whatsoever without prior written consent of the author, except as provided by the United States of America copyright law.

Published by Advantage, Charleston, South Carolina.
Member of Advantage Media Group.

ADVANTAGE is a registered trademark, and the Advantage colophon is a trademark of Advantage Media Group, Inc.

Printed in the United States of America.

10 9 8 7 6 5 4 3 2 1

ISBN: 978-1-59932-925-3
LCCN: 2018939809

Book design by Megan Elger.

This publication is designed to provide accurate and authoritative information in regard to the subject matter covered. It is sold with the understanding that the publisher is not engaged in rendering legal, accounting, or other professional services. If legal advice or other expert assistance is required, the services of a competent professional person should be sought.

TreeNeutral™

Advantage Media Group is proud to be a part of the Tree Neutral® program. Tree Neutral offsets the number of trees consumed in the production and printing of this book by taking proactive steps such as planting trees in direct proportion to the number of trees used to print books. To learn more about Tree Neutral, please visit **www.treeneutral.com**.

Advantage Media Group is a publisher of business, self-improvement, and professional development books and online learning. We help entrepreneurs, business leaders, and professionals share their Stories, Passion, and Knowledge to help others Learn & Grow. Do you have a manuscript or book idea that you would like us to consider for publishing? Please visit **advantagefamily.com** or call **1.866.775.1696**.

TABLE OF CONTENTS

ACKNOWLEDGMENTS

No book would happen without the help of a great team. First, I am grateful for my wife and partner, Christina, for giving up time, resources, and energy for allowing me to work on this book and get it into your hands. Also to my wonderful children Anthony, Arabella, and Vince for giving up their time with me to complete this book as well.

I have to thank everyone at Geraci LLP for their input, thoughts, reviews, and edits of this book! Without them this wouldn't have happened. Nema, this is the book you never wanted but knew we needed. Kevin, you knew this was the book you wanted and needed and never thought it would come to fruition.

Most importantly, I have to thank my clients and partners throughout this journey who have believed in me since I opened the firm's doors over ten years ago. There are way too many to be named in these short acknowledgements, but you know who you are. I wouldn't be here without you, and please never for a minute doubt that I have forgotten it. Thank you for your belief in us as a firm. I hope this is a small token back to all of you so you can continue to educate everyone on the benefits of non-conventional lending and helping so many people find financial freedom wherever they are.

Cheers,
Anthony Geraci, Esq.
Irvine, California

DON'T JUST SIT THERE— DO SOMETHING!

Alice: "Would you tell me, please, which way I ought to go from here?"

The Cheshire Cat: "That depends a good deal on where you want to get to."

Alice: "I don't much care where."

The Cheshire Cat: "Then it doesn't matter which way you go."

Alice: "... so long as I get SOMEWHERE."

The Cheshire Cat: "Oh, you're sure to do that, if you only walk long enough."

I probably shouldn't be living the life I'm living. I grew up poor. My family moved nearly every year as my dad looked for work. I was a middle-school dropout—and no one at the school noticed. This is not the standard childhood of a law firm founding partner and successful investor.

But I had one thing going for me. I was—and am—driven. If I set a goal, I find a way to make it happen. I know beyond a shadow of a doubt that if I only walk long enough, I'll reach that goal. And I had a single, overarching goal through most of my life; it wasn't anything esoteric or high-brow.

I simply wanted to make money and do deals.

From a very young age, I knew where I wanted to go. I knew where I wanted to end up. My challenge was to find the path to take me there.

In looking for that path, I ended up going down some rather winding, nontraditional, and less-traveled roads. I spent the years others spend in high school reading whatever interested me—and lots of subjects interested me—and working at whatever jobs I could get. There were times before I was technically old enough to work when I had to find employers willing to skirt child labor laws.

Because I didn't go to high school, I qualified for college via the GED. My eclectic reading served me well, and I qualified for a scholarship that allowed me to attend Auburn (after spending a couple of years at the community college to take care of prerequisites at a reasonable cost). I then rotated through five different majors before landing on the one that felt right and made me feel like I was moving in the right direction. After undergrad, I chose to go to law school in California—because I thought lawyers made money, but also because I just wanted to live in California. Often the right decision is based on criteria as simple as just wanting to do it.

Keeping focused on the goal in mind is crucial. How you get there isn't nearly as important as the fact that you are, indeed, getting there.

My nonlinear route to success taught me some important lessons that could be applicable to almost anyone. Those lessons were:

1. Wandering off the beaten path can allow you to stumble on solutions you might not have seen if you had followed the well-worn path others have trodden.

2. Move on quickly from nonproductive enterprises, without looking back.

3. There are more than one way of doing things.

Each of these lessons has played a large part in my success, both as a law firm founder and as an investor, because they've allowed me to often cut straight to the heart of the problem and find the best solutions. Sometimes those solutions are obvious from the beginning, but more often than not they are only obvious if you are looking at the situation from a different angle, or if your mind tends to put puzzle pieces together in a nonstandard way.

Back in 2008, at the beginning of the recession, I couldn't have dreamed that one of my untrodden paths would lead me to nonconventional lending. I couldn't have dreamed about it, because I didn't know about it. After being introduced to this investment vehicle by a broker who thought I'd be a good investor, I've come to believe that it is the best-kept secret in the investment world.

Yes, it takes more personal involvement than buying mutual funds or real estate investment trust (REIT) stocks over the Internet. And it probably takes a bit more capital than some other, more mainstream investments. But the upside is so up, it's hard to believe that more investors—many more investors—aren't involved.

This is an investment that pays off in good times and bad. It's appropriate for investors with $15,000 to invest, as well as those with $150,000 or $1.5 million to invest. It takes advantage of one of the best cash-flow asset classes in the world—real estate—while providing the stability of fixed-income bonds. And it allows the investor to be in control of the investment.

I am convinced that more people would jump into this investment sector if they only knew about it. So, I've set myself a goal: spread the word and explain the benefits of non-conventional lending to anyone who wants to secure a better, wealthier life for themselves and their family. Isn't that everybody? (Anyone who says being wealthy doesn't bring happiness has never been poor.)

And you know what happens when I set a goal—I keep walking until I reach it. I decided that one of the most efficient, straight-path ways of reaching that goal and helping investors understand this hidden gem of a sector was to write this book. I'll take you through my first investments to give you an idea of how things can go wrong and, mainly, how things that usually go right. This book will take you through the hows and whys of an investment sector that I want to bring out of the shadows and place on stage in the middle of lots of flood lights.

I'm not alone. Tony Robbins—well-known author, entrepreneur, philanthropist, and life coach, who is often credited with the words-to-live-by mantra, "If you do what you've always done, you'll get what you've always gotten"—invests in this space, as noted in his book, *Money: Master the Game.*

> If senior housing seems out of reach, another strategy in real estate is lending your money with a first trust deed [non-conventional loan] as security. In the chapter on asset allocation, I'll describe to you an example of how

investors who need money will take short-term loans at high rates—for example, a one-year loan for 8 percent or 10 percent, and you get the first trust deed as collateral. When done effectively, you can loan, say, $50,000 on a $100,000 home, or $500,000 on a $1 million home, and the property could drop 50 percent, and you'd still be in good shape. While others are collecting 3 and 4 percent returns, you're getting 8 to 10 percent.[1]

Investing in the non-conventional lending space is a great way to stop investing the way you've always done so you can get more than you've always gotten. In addition to Robbins, more and more successful people, including Sanjay Gupta and Orel Hershiser, as well as family offices and high-net-worth individuals, are investing in the non-conventional lending space because they see what I see—the opportunity to achieve above-average, fixed-income returns via loans secured by something that is never worth nothing: real estate.

This book will open a new investment sector for you, but it will also leave you with some homework. If this sector is going to take its rightful place in investors' portfolios, we need to have more voices involved. We need to share our concerns and our successes. We need to develop a group of best practices that will give the industry credibility while also making it a welcoming place for newcomers and experienced lenders alike. Right now, the sector is dominated by individual brokers and investors who do one-off deals and rarely share data with each other. We need people like you to help us look behind the screen.

You are probably thinking, "Okay, this sounds too good to be true." This saying came from writers like Mark Twain, who in *Huck-*

---

1   Tony Robbins, *Money: Master the Game*, New York: Simon & Schuster, 2016.

leberry Finn wrote, "It's too good for true, honey, it's too good for true." Listen to me, as a lawyer and as someone who has done non-conventional lending for his own personal investment for years, and I will teach you how these investments are too good to be ignored and how to protect yourself if something were to happen. If, after you read this book, you are still hesitant to become an investor, let me know why. What would make the industry more attractive? If you like what you read, I also want to know that. Are there specific benefits you find most attractive? In other words, I want to hear your reactions. Only by listening to those on the outside looking in will we be able to open the doors wider and get you all inside.

So, it's time to turn the page and begin moving along the path that can take you to your goal of financial security. Non-conventional lending is calling your name.

After each chapter, we're going to have key takeaways for the chapter you just read, as well as tasks for you to work on. I want this book to not just sit on your shelf—I want you to take action, and take control of your portfolio!

KEY TAKEAWAYS FROM THE INTRODUCTION:

1. There is no one path to success.
2. Non-conventional lending offers a path.
3. While not a heavily trodden path, Tony Robbins and other successful investors have found non-conventional lending to be a great way to earn steady, high-yield returns.

TAKE ACTION *NOW*

Go to http://www.nonconlendingguide.com/intro for updated

information, resources, and secrets.

KEY QUESTION:

How comfortable are you with your investment portfolio?

CHAPTER 1

LOOKING FOR RETURNS— BUT FINDING JUNK

We all have friends like John and Julie, who seemed to be doing everything right. Maybe you are them. They live within their means. They don't overspend. They have a money market account equal to four months of living expenses. They have a savings account and 529 plans for their kids' college expenses. They have 401(k) plans plus other investments for their retirement. But when it came time to pay for college, they and their kids needed to take out loans that they are still paying back twenty years later. Now, as they near retirement, it is obvious they don't have anywhere near enough to cover the lifestyle they had planned for their golden years.

It wasn't supposed to be this way. Their own parents had been able to pay for their children's college, their daughter's wedding, a comfortable lifestyle, and still save enough to retire to a golf community in Florida. What's wrong with John and Julie that they can't match their parents' financial acumen?

In truth, nothing is wrong. They simply found themselves caught in a time when income and savings have struggled to keep up with increasing expenses. Their parents probably had a pension to provide income during retirement. College, especially in-state public schools, can be just a few thousand dollars a year. A mortgage didn't take up more than a third of their monthly income—it was likely less than a quarter.

For example, the average annual cost of tuition, room, and board at a private, four-year university during the 2014–2015 school year was $34,193, according to the US Department of Education's National Center for Education Statistics.[2] The average cost for a year at a public university was $16,482. This compares to an average cost of $13,340 for a private education and $5,243 at a public school for the 1990–1991 academic year. This comes out to a 156 percent increase for private education over the past twenty years, or a 214 percent increase for the "less expensive" public option.

When books, supplies, transportation, personal expenses, and other fees are added in, the costs are even higher. In its most recent survey of college pricing, the College Board reports that a moderate college budget for an in-state public college for the 2017–2018 academic year averaged $25,290, a moderate budget for a year at a private college averaged $50,900.[3] And it's not getting cheaper. Vanguard's research shows that college prices have increased 6 percent a

2   "Average Cost of College Tuition," Statistic Brain, last modified June 7, 2017, https://www.statisticbrain.com/average-cost-of-college-tuition/.

3   "Average Estimated Undergraduate Budgets, 2017–18," Trends in Higher Education, CollegeBoard, https://trends.collegeboard.org/college-pricing/figures-tables/average-estimated-undergraduate-budgets-2017-18.

year.[4] By the time this book turns eighteen years old, that means a college education could cost $120,000 a year.[5]

It isn't just education costs that have outpaced inflation. Healthcare costs have exploded in the past twenty years, as we hear every time we turn on the news. In 1997, healthcare expenses in the United States averaged $4,345 per person, and by 2016, we were spending $10,348 per person.[6] This is a whopping 138 percent increase. If healthcare costs had just been driven by inflation, the country would be averaging only $6,627 per person.

Need more examples of the obstacles facing families who are saving for retirement, or even a rainy day? How about housing prices? We all need a place to live. The average price of a new home in July 1997 was $175,500. In July 2017, that average had risen to $372,400.[7] If the price increase was simply a function of inflation, that 2017 home would have only been $267,663.

Meanwhile, median personal income during that twenty-year period has risen just a bit more than inflation. Weekly median personal income in 1997 was $503. By mid-2017, it had risen to $859.[8] If it had risen only through inflation, the 2017 weekly median income would be $768. So, income has also grown more than inflation, but that 71 percent increase in income doesn't begin

---

4   "What's the average cost of college?" Vanguard, https://investor.vanguard.com/college-savings-plans/average-cost-of-college.

5   Vanessa Wong, "In 18 years, a college degree could cost about $500,000," CNBC, https://www.cnbc.com/2017/03/17/in-18-years-a-college-degree-could-cost-about-500000.html.

6   Centers for Medicare and Medicaid Services, https://www.cms.gov/Research-Statistics-Data-and-Systems/Statistics-Trends-and-Reports/NationalHealthExpendData/NationalHealthAccountsHistorical.html.

7   US Census Bureau, "Median and Average Sales Prices of New Homes Sold in United States," https://www.census.gov/construction/nrs/pdf/uspricemon.pdf.

8   Bureau of Labor Statistics, "Labor Force Statistics from the Current Population Survey," https://www.bls.gov/cps/earnings.htm.

to cover the 214 percent increase in public college expenses, the 112 percent increase in the sales price of a new home, or the 138 percent jump in healthcare costs.

It's no wonder, then, that people are finding it hard to save for college, retirement, and other major life expenses. When people have less disposable income because they are focused on paying for necessities, savings get pushed to the side.

According to Fidelity Investments's tenth Annual College Indicator Study, 70 percent of parents intend to pay 100 percent of their children's college tuition.[9] However, by the time their children graduate from high school (or complete the GED, as I did), the average parent can only cover 29 percent of the cost of a four-year college.[10]

Saving for retirement is even harder. If you've been listening to conventional wisdom, you know most people will need about $1 million in savings and investments to fund a comfortable retirement. A Legg Mason survey found that higher-income individuals believe they will need at least $2.5 million to maintain their lifestyle.[11]

Despite knowing that they need around $1 million for a comfortable retirement, 47 percent of Americans have less than $25,000 saved when they retire. Approximately 80 percent of Americans retire with less than $250,000 in their nest egg, according to the Employee Benefit Research Institute.[12]

---

9   "Tenth Annual College Savings Indicator: Executive Summary of Key Findings," Fidelity Investments, 2016.

10   Ibid.

11   "US Investors Need $2.5 Million for Retirement," Legg Mason, http://www. multivu.com/players/English/7466451-legg-mason-global-investor-survey/

12   "2017 Retirement Confidence Survey: 2017 Results," EBRI Issue Brief, Employee Benefit Research Institute, (March 2017): https://www.ebri.org/surveys/ rcs/2017/.

It's time to stop doing what we've always done. At some point, life stops happening to you, and you start happening to life. If you are going to reach your goals, you have to have a plan. You have to stop doing things that aren't working and find things that are. For me and some others, non-conventional lending is working very well.

A BETTER WAY TO INVEST

When it comes to putting together an investment portfolio to cover the cost of retirement, most people rely on the stock market to supply growth, while also holding fixed-income bonds and dividend stocks for cash flow. If we could trust that the equities markets would always go up, investing in stocks would be a no-brainer strategy. Those who invested heavily in stocks after the Great Recession, or who managed to hold onto their investments through the recession, experienced one of the great bull runs in the history of the market. But that bull run came after one of the deepest crashes in the past century. Private investors who were getting ready to pay for their child's college or buy a house or begin their retirement in 2008 or 2009 suddenly found their stock portfolios in negative territory. Many had to continue working, downsize their house, and adjust their lifestyle. Relying on a volatile investment like securities for needs such as income after retirement doesn't make sense. Investors need a more stable source of income.

Fixed-income markets are certainly stable, no question about that. In a world where ten-year treasuries have been returning less than 3 percent during the past decade—and at times after the recession, they were coming in closer to 1 percent than 2 percent—investors are not going to fund a comfortable retirement via the bond market. In fact, because most investors are told to keep at least 20 percent to 30 percent of their portfolios in fixed-income instruments—with that percentage rising as they age—I'd argue that traditional investors are actually hurting their chances of reaching their financial goals, because the returns on these investments are pulling down the entire portfolio.

Compare your returns with inflation, which is generally defined as the increase in prices and the fall of the purchasing value of your hard-earned dollars. As of September 2017, the inflation rate for the previous twelve months was 2.2 percent.[13] That means that if you're earning 2 percent on your investments, you are *losing money*!

It's obvious that what we have traditionally been doing to fund our retirements and save for other large goals isn't working any more. We need to look at alternative investments if we are going to reach our long-term goals.

Non-conventional lending is one of those alternative investments. It has the reputation of being risky, but much of that reputation comes from the subprime days, when banks lent to anyone with a pulse, and fraud was rampant in the industry. Back then, it was often a joke in the industry that *everyone* owned a catering company and made $10,000 a month, thus qualifying for "stated income loans," which Wall Street was only too happy to include in their high-flying mortgage securitizations. Today, with the addition of the SAFE Mortgage Licensing Act (which prompts states to establish minimum standards for the licensing and registration of mortgage loan originators, among other things to protect the consumer) and other laws, non-conventional lending is really not any riskier than other investments. Think about it. Banks and credit unions have used mortgages secured by a real asset to drive their profits for decades. They view

---

13   US Inflation Calculator, "Current US Inflation Rates: 2008–2018," http://www. usinflationcalculator.com/inflation/current-inflation-rates/.

these loans as the safest—and most profitable—income vehicle they have. If staid, conservative institutions such as banks and credit unions rely on mortgages, it only makes sense that private investors can, too.

Far from being extra risky, non-conventional lending is often safer than more traditional investment classes, for a number of reasons. First, the notes that non-conventional lenders hold on properties tend to be written at a pretty conservative loan-to-value ratio—generally around 75 percent of the purchase price. Some particularly conservative investors only lend up to 65 percent. That offers a lot of protection in getting your principal back. Second, if you lend to experienced property investors, these investments are safer than other fixed-income investments, because they are secured by *real* property. This security is not going to disappear overnight. Finally, just like your mom and dad taught you, look at the character of the borrower. Lend to good people, and you won't have issues with them later.

I can't emphasize this last point enough. In a world of spreadsheets, return-on-investment metrics, and P&L statements, we sometimes forget that we are working with real people. And real people come in all sorts of ethical packages. You want to deal with the ones in the good packages. You want the ones who not only take their contractual obligations seriously but who also do the right thing when the right thing is called for.

Warren Buffett has built an empire on only dealing with good people. He has often been quoted as saying one of the secrets to his success was that he "learned to go into business only with people I like, trust, and admire."

One of the real advantages of non-conventional lending is that you are in control. You choose whom you are lending to. No matter how great the numbers look, if you're not comfortable with the person behind those numbers, you can (and should) say, "Not this time."

Going back to the Warren Buffett bucket of quotes, "You only have to do a very few things right in your life, so long as you don't do too many things wrong." Investing with someone you don't trust is doing something wrong. Avoid doing that, and your chances of success skyrocket.

Every investment carries risk—that's why you get paid interest for making the investment—but when it comes to comparing the levels of risk you'll encounter when investing in different asset classes, I'd argue that having 50 percent or more of your portfolio in the stock market is the riskiest investment you can make. People will investigate a company and decide it is a good, strong, growing enterprise, so they buy that company's stock. Now, the company's value doesn't usually change daily, because its true value is based on revenues, inventory, assets, and other attributes that simply don't change very quickly. Yet you see stock prices go up and down daily—in fact, they are usually changing by the minute. Your research does nothing to help you control for the fear and rumors that cause a stock to jump or fall day-to-day. In the non-conventional world, you're not going to see that kind of volatility. You might see properties go up or down 5 percent to 10 percent, but even that is rare given that these loans tend to cover months rather than years and that real estate simply is not very volatile (the housing crisis of 2007–2008 notwithstanding). Consider what happened after the British people voted for Brexit, which had no impact on corporate profits in the United States. The very next day, the US stock market dropped 3 percent, with no other major event happening. The stock market is based as much on fear and greed as it is on smarts.

One of the things I learned early in life—when my family sometimes moved more than once a year as my father sought work—is that you have to be flexible. Being able to let go of preconceived ideas of what a school would be like helped me adjust and make friends. Being able to let go of preconceived ideas of a stocks-and-bonds portfolio and trying something new will serve you as well as it did me. I learned that there is more than one path to get to where you need to be. Non-conventional lending is an unorthodox path to boost portfolio returns, but it is one I think you'll find very profitable.

Throughout the rest of this book, I'll show you how to take part in this investment class, which is providing double-digit returns with controllable risks. It's a sector that very few know about, but it's time to bring it out of the shadows and let non-conventional lenders and investors realize the returns they need to meet their goals.

DEFINITIONS

There are a number of words used throughout this book that you may not be familiar with. Please use this as a constant reference in your non-conventional lending business to refer to. For more definitions, check out the Non-Conventional Lending Guide at http://www.nonconlendingguide.com.

after repair value (ARV)—This is the estimated value of a property after rehab work has been done. It is often used to procure a loan to make those repairs.

balloon loans—A balloon loan is a loan that only contemplates getting interest-only payments (payments that will not pay any outstanding principal on the note) and, at the maturity date, the borrower will repay the entire principal of the loan.

bond rating—Bonds are rated by a rating agency, such as Standard

& Poor's, Moody's, or Fitch, on how likely the bond issuer is to meet payment obligations and repay principal in a timely manner. These ratings are given out as grades, with AAA being the best and anything below BBB– being considered junk or noninvestment grade. Typically, the lower the grade, the higher the risk of default, but also the higher the return if payments are made.

borrower—A borrower is anyone who takes something from someone else with the intention of returning it. A borrower is, for the purpose of this book, someone who receives money from a non-conventional lender, with the intention of returning the principal with interest.

default—If the borrower fails to repay the loan, he or she is said to be in default. It is at this stage that you will decide whether to restructure the loan with the hopes that it will get paid in full under the new terms, or to take over the property.

comps—"Comps" is the shortened term for "*comparisons.*" When doing their due diligence, lenders look at what comparable properties have sold for and compare them to the property being offered as collateral to determine the value of the property.

Dodd-Frank Wall Street Reform and Consumer Protection Act (Dodd-Frank)—Implemented after the financial crisis of 2008–2009, this Act places limits on the amount and kinds of risks that banks can take when making investments.

fixed-income—A fixed-income is an investment that provides a quantifiable and predictable return on investment.

foreclose—This is the act of taking possession of a property as a result of the borrower failing to keep up his or her payments.

Global Financial Crisis (GFC)—The GFC occurred during 2007–2008, when a burst housing bubble and unwise securitizations caused the collapse of credit markets and led to the Great Recession.

loan-to-value (LTV)—A percentage calculation that is a measurement of the risk the non-conventional lender will take on a particular loan. The loan-to-value ratio is calculated by dividing the principal balance of the promissory note by the value of the property.

non-conventional lender—A person who lends money to a third party with the expectation of making a profit. That person is probably you. They may also be called a *private moneylender* or *hard moneylender*.

promissory note—A promissory note is the promise a borrower makes to repay the lender a certain sum of money plus interest.

return on investment (ROI)—ROI is a measure of profitability. There are many ways to determine it, but the easiest is to take your net profits and divide it by your total investment. For instance, if you invested $50,000 and had a net profit of $10,000, your ROI would be .2, or 20 percent.

securitization—A bank reduces the risk of providing mortgages by bundling the mortgages it holds into a mortgage-backed financial instrument—a security—and selling it to investors on Wall Street. Investors in these securities require that the mortgages meet certain credit standards, which means the bank is limited as to how flexible it can be in providing mortgages to the community.

SAFE Mortgage Licensing Act—This Act was a regulation implemented after the 2007 housing crisis to encourage states to set minimum licensing requirements for mortgage loan providers. In addition, all mortgage loan originators working for banks and some other national lenders must register with the National Mortgage Licensing System. It is typically referred to as the SAFE Act.

subprime—Investors with a damaged credit history or who do not qualify for traditional loans are considered subprime. Loans made to this cohort will have a higher interest rate to pay for the increased risk.

yield—The yield is the income return an investor receives from making an investment. It is designated as a percentage and is typically paid out to investors via interest or dividends.

KEY TAKEAWAYS FROM CHAPTER 1:

1. Inflation and cost of services/homes have far outpaced increases in wages and income. Keeping money in a savings account is actually *losing* money due to inflation.
2. The old ways of investing won't help you accomplish your goals.
3. Non-conventional lending is one strategy that can help increase your income to pay for the increased expenses.

TAKE ACTION *NOW*

1. Talk to your investment adviser about non-conventional loans. Did you know that non-conventional loans are a $1 trillion business?
2. How can non-conventional loans fit in your overall investment portfolio?

Go to http://www.nonconlendingguide.com/chapter1 for updated information, resources, and secrets.

KEY QUESTION:

If the stock market were to tank like it did in 2007–2009, are you still fully protected to reach your retirement goals?

CHAPTER 2

THE DAWN OF A NEW INVESTMENT SECTOR

Non-conventional lending might be the second-oldest profession in the world. Stories of ancient Greece and Rome often involve characters who lend money in exchange for a physical or real item. (We would probably call them pawnbrokers today.) One of the more well-known stories in the Bible revolves around moneylenders in the Temple. Move into the Middle Ages, and you come across indentured servants, who paid off their debts by working for the rich family that lent them money. *The Merchant of Venice* and its Shylock, a poor stereotype and caricature of a private lender that has unfortunately found its way down through the centuries, brought moneylending front and center. Despite its long history, however, most investors have never thought to make private lending a part of their investment portfolios. It's simply not on their radar. Yet it should be. The benefits are too great to ignore.

WHAT IS NON-CONVENTIONAL LENDING?

Non-conventional lending, also known as private money-lending or hard moneylending, involves a nonbank loan from an investor, such as yourself, to a third-party, such as me, with the expectation of realizing a profit when the loan is paid off.

Non-conventional lending is essentially a less regulated mortgage supplied by a private investor or broker rather than a bank or mortgage company. Because there are fewer regulations, investors are free to lend to borrowers who don't qualify for a traditional loan. Borrowers can have many reasons for avoiding a bank. They could be self-employed and lack the documentation needed for a bank loan, or maybe their credit history is too short or has a one-time blip. Maybe they are looking for something short-term, and it's not worth their time to do all the paperwork required by a bank. And yes, sometimes they are a real risk of default.

Here's an illustration: A very successful, young entrepreneur was buying a $4 million house. (A few Internet start-ups were very, very good to some of their founders.) He was going to put $3 million down, so this was basically a 25 percent LTV mortgage request. He should have easily qualified for a bank loan. But at this point in his life, he didn't have a credit history, because he had never needed credit. He had spent the few years of his adult life in front of a computer screen, developing a platform and building a business; rather than buying consumer products on credit, he paid for whatever he needed in cash. More importantly to a bank, an ex-partner had won an $853 judgment against him. He said he would rather die than pay that judgment. The bank rejected him because of that judgment and lack of credit history. That's where the banks have no common sense sometimes. If I was the bank, I'd want that loan regardless. Forget that $800 judgment, and look at the whole picture, which is what a non-conventional lender can do. Here was an ultra-successful businessman, who had the capital behind him to make the purchase and refused to pay the judgment based on principle, not because he couldn't afford to do so. That should have been a no-brainer loan for the bank. It certainly was for the private lender, who stepped in to make the loan and ended up with a very nice interest rate and profit.

Another roadblock to traditional financing might be in the property itself. Unconventional property purchases are the bread and butter of the non-conventional lender. These are the properties that support the industry. Banks want nothing to do with non-owner-occupied rental units or speculative rehab projects. It can also be hard to find bank financing for small, mixed-use properties or land purchases if you are not a large, established developer.

The bottom line is that non-conventional lenders are not terribly concerned about the reasons the borrower is unable or unwilling to get bank financing. They are really only interested in (1) the liquidation value of the property, because that is what secures the loan—as long as the property can be sold for more than the amount of the loan, the investor's capital is protected; (2) the character of the borrower—does he or she have the integrity to make the payments; and (3) the experience and skill-set of the borrower—can the borrower accomplish what he or she set out to do?

To understand how this rapidly growing investment category fits into an investor's portfolio today, it is helpful to look back at how it has evolved over time.

A (VERY) BRIEF HISTORY OF LENDING

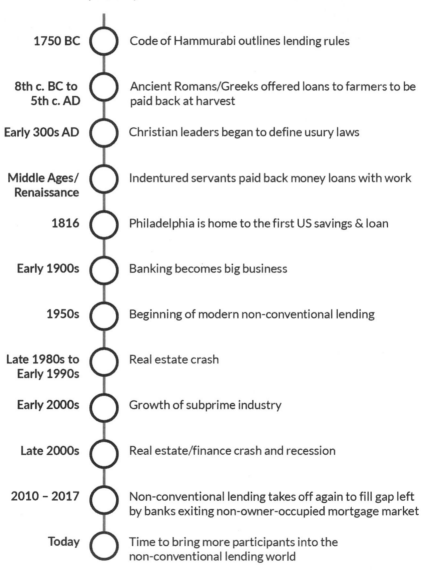

1750 BC	Code of Hammurabi outlines lending rules
8th c. BC to 5th c. AD	Ancient Romans/Greeks offered loans to farmers to be paid back at harvest
Early 300s AD	Christian leaders began to define usury laws
Middle Ages/ Renaissance	Indentured servants paid back money loans with work
1816	Philadelphia is home to the first US savings & loan
Early 1900s	Banking becomes big business
1950s	Beginning of modern non-conventional lending
Late 1980s to Early 1990s	Real estate crash
Early 2000s	Growth of subprime industry
Late 2000s	Real estate/finance crash and recession
2010 – 2017	Non-conventional lending takes off again to fill gap left by banks exiting non-owner-occupied mortgage market
Today	Time to bring more participants into the non-conventional lending world

We know that non-conventional lending, which involved return of the item loaned plus some type of interest, goes back at least 3700 years, because it is mentioned in the Code of Hammurabi, which dates to the end of his reign—around 1750 BC. Babylonians and other peoples of Mesopotamia who wanted to lend money, crops, or land for profit only had to look to Laws 49 and 50 to see how to do it legally.[14]

> "If a man has taken money from a merchant and has given a field prepared for corn or sesame to the merchant and has stated to him: 'Cultivate the field, and heap up take and keep the corn or sesame which may be raised,' if a cultivator raises corn or sesame on that field, at the harvest it is the owner of the field who shall take the corn or the sesame, which may be raised on the field and shall give corn for his money, which he has received from the merchant, and the interest on it and the costs of the cultivation to the merchant.

> "If he has lent a cultivated field (of corn) or a field of sesame, it is the owner of the field who shall take the corn or the sesame which may be raised on the field and shall repay the money and the interest thereon to the merchant."[15]

With recorded person-to-person lending stretching back to well before Roman civilization, it's safe to assume people were lending and receiving some sort of compensation for their troubles well before that. I wouldn't be surprised if some of the paintings found

---

14   K.V. Nagarajan, "The Code of Hammurabi: an Economic Interpretation," http://academic.kellogg.edu/williamsjon/Hammurabi.htm.

15   Ibid.

on cave walls depicted private loans. It seems obvious that lending and borrowing are part of human nature. And along with the instinct to lend comes the preference to receive some sort of compensation for that loan. It was corn or sesame in 1750 BC; today we look for specific interest or dividends to cover the cost of risk.

LENDING IN MODERN TIMES

Lending started as a private enterprise, with neighbor helping neighbor, farmer helping farmer, and families helping families. Most of the history of lending follows this model. But as we grew from small tribes and villages to large cities, states, provinces, and countries, lending became more institutionalized. In modern times, lending became the purview of banks, which relied on the interest returns from lending out deposits to fund their businesses.

By the early 1900s, banking was big business. As the economy grew and expanded, banks loaned more and more money. The more capital they loaned, the more money they made. But all this exuberance came to a crushing end as the Great Depression, which in part was due to the overextension of bank lending to stockbrokers,[16] brought everyone to their knees.

The Great Depression should have been the wake-up call to end all wake-up calls. You would have thought that bankers would have learned their lesson about extending credit without strict underwriting and adequate margin requirements. You would have thought wrong. This boom-and-bust of good times followed by contrite promises to do things differently in the future seems to play out every seventeen years or so. We just can't help ourselves.

---

16   Peter Fortune, "Margin Requirements, Margin Loans, and Margin Rates: Practice and Principles – analysis of history of margin credit regulations – Statistical Data Included," *New England Economic Review*, September/October 2000: 20–44.

But we do try. In the late 1950s, following the boom of the postwar decade, we reshaped the mortgage industry by implementing more restrictive and standardized requirements for mortgage borrowers. With the tightening of lending requirements, we saw the beginnings of a truly professional mortgage industry, and we also saw the real beginnings of the non-conventional lending industry in the United States.

These stricter lending guidelines resulted in some borrowers being shut out of traditional bank mortgages. This drove many commercial property developers and owners to non-conventional lenders to finance their properties and projects. Non-conventional lenders became a trusted source of finance for the next twenty years or so—until the real estate crash of the late 1980s and 1990s hit. Remember my mention of the bankers failing to learn their lesson? Well, non-conventional lenders were also lured in by the prospect of higher and higher returns. Because they had overvalued the properties they were lending on, they lost their investments when property values fell.

As we came out of the GFC, which began with the housing crisis in 2007, everyone promised that we would never again see the easy credit policies that led to the crash. As they say, never say never. Just ten years later, we were already seeing credit requirements loosening, mortgage securitizations returning, and the low–down-payment loan making a comeback. Much of this can be traced to the decade-long run of historically low interest rates. It's hard for a bank to make money when it can only charge 3 percent interest on a mortgage. But loosen the credit requirements, and voila—banks can charge higher interest rates to a wider universe of borrowers who don't meet the standard requirements. Humans are not very good at resisting temptation, and the temptation to make money by charging higher interest rates to less creditworthy borrowers is real.

TODAY'S NON-CONVENTIONAL LENDING

After the real estate crashes of the 1980s and 1990s, non-conventional lenders learned to be more conservative with property valuations. The length of loans and interest rates grew slowly and responsibly, as participants became comfortable with the risks and benefits. It was still a very small niche in a very big investment world, but it was chugging along. Then came the GFC of 2007–2009, and the non-conventional financial industry found its stride.

Alternative and Subprime Lending Before the Crash of 2007

To understand non-conventional lending today, we have to understand the rise and fall of subprime lending. While it's hard to pinpoint which company started subprime lending, there are several that can serve as an example. New Century Financial is one of the better-known lenders that went from originating more than $40 billion in loans to bankruptcy nearly overnight. One of my previous clients, Bob Cole, used to tell me stories of how he, Brad Morrice, and Ed Gotschall started New Century out of a car. The company made its first loan in 1996 and quickly went public. Within two years, it "had grown to 1,151 employees, had 111 offices, originated $2 billion in mortgages and made $17.7 million in net profits."[17] By 2006, it was the second-largest subprime lender in the country, with Option One Mortgage being the first.

New Century focused on the subprime market, because it was an underserved niche with higher-than-normal returns. These borrowers generally did not meet the credit standards of traditional financial institutions. Maybe they hadn't been at their job long enough, or maybe their income-to-debt ratio was a little out of whack. Maybe

---

17   Barry Nielsen, "The Rise and Demise of New Century Financial," Investopedia, http://www.investopedia.com/articles/07/new-century.asp.

their credit history was too short or not pristine. Whatever the reason, traditional banks were not willing to lend, but New Century was.

New Century was also willing to forego some of the traditional protections in mortgage lending, such as a 20 percent down payment and proof of income. Because real estate values were increasing by double digits every year, they began offering nothing-down, no-documentation, adjustable, and interest-only mortgages. The idea was that the borrower just had to pay the interest for three to five years, and because values were appreciating so quickly, they would then have plenty of equity to refinance and qualify for a lower-interest, standard bank loan.

The demand for New Century's product exceeded anyone's expectation. In its heyday, Chase and Wells Fargo both issued nine-figure credit lines to New Century, and New Century would repackage these loans with the help of the big banks and sell them on Wall Street. Yet, one year after ranking second in subprime mortgage origination, New Century filed for Chapter 11 bankruptcy, a victim of rising interest rates and an overwhelming number of defaults by borrowers who had taken out adjustable-rate or interest-only mortgages and couldn't keep up when the payments adjusted to market rate. Add to that an overheated housing market whose bubble burst and left no more equity for borrowers to refinance out of, and they just simply couldn't afford the payments. The traditional banks might have been on to something with their credit and underwriting standards.

Why am I telling you the story of New Century, which is really the story of many lenders in the early 2000s? Because, during this time, non-conventional lending was focused on a part of the credit stack even lower than subprime. This really was a dangerous place to play. Borrowers who had any kind of job—or the prospect of a job, or no job at all if they were willing to say they had one—could get a mortgage through a subprime broker. The joke used to be that if you could fog a mirror, you could get a mortgage.

HOW CREDIT SCORE AFFECTED LENDING IN EARLY 2000s

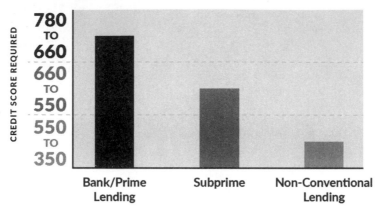

SOURCE OF MORTGAGE LOAN

As you can see above, non-conventional lending during the subprime days was limited with regard to the quality of the borrower. Due to subprime lenders' proliferation and ability to sell their loans to Wall Street, true non-conventional lending found itself generally compressed and serving the bottom tier of the credit spectrum.

Non-Conventional Lending After the Subprime Crash

SUBPRIME MORTGAGE ORIGINATIONS

In 2006, $600 billion of subprime loans were originated, most of which were securitized. That year, subprime lending accounted for 23.5% of all mortgage originations.

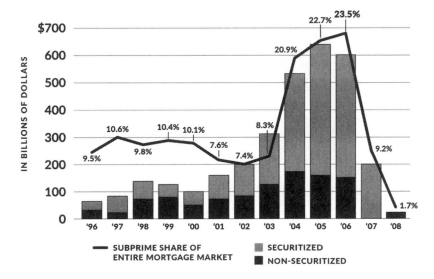

NOTE: Percent securitized is defined as subprime securities issued by originations in a given year. In 2007, securities issued exceeded originations.

SOURCE: Inside Mortgage Finance

After the subprime crash, private lenders were able to move up in the credit stack, because subprime originators were forced out of the market. Due to Wall Street shying away from securitized mortgages, the concern over the SAFE Mortgage Licensing Act and Dodd-Frank, and the tightening of bank lending standards during this time, the credit stack now looked like this:

HOW CREDIT SCORE AFFECTED LENDING IN LATE 2000s

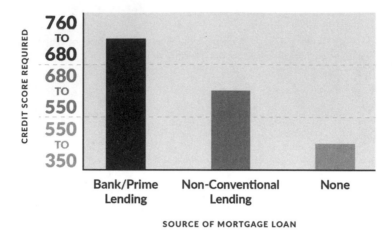

SOURCE OF MORTGAGE LOAN

As subprime was eliminated, you can see the credit stack moved upward, and anyone wanting to make non-conventional loans would be dealing with a more creditworthy universe. Unfortunately, it also meant that certain segments of the population were no longer eligible for credit, even from private lenders.

THE RISE OF NON-CONVENTIONAL LENDING

We can point to three primary drivers for the increase in interest in non-conventional financing since the crash.

The Rehab Boom

First of all, there was a jump in the speculative rehabbing, or *flipping*, of private residences for profit. Flipping homes (i.e., the act of buying a house, improving it by updating, repairing, remodeling, and then reselling, hopefully at a profit) has been around a long time. It became particularly popular in the aftermath of the recession, circa

2009–2017, when a large inventory of single-family houses and condos came on the market due to foreclosures from the subprime crash. Buying houses to flip became so popular that home-improvement TV networks began featuring the exploits of attractive couples and their professional rehab adventures. These are some of the most popular shows on those channels, and they have inspired thousands of non-professional flippers to try their hands at rehabbing a house for profit. Both professional and novice rehabbers often need the quick, short-term financing that private lending is known for, as seen on the shows, when cost overruns require a quick infusion of cash, or the rehabbers need an investor to front the costs of purchase.

Federal and State Regulations

In an effort to prevent a repeat of the housing crisis caused by over-enthusiastic bank lending, the SAFE Act, the Dodd-Frank Wall Street Reform and Consumer Protection Act, the Volcker Rule, the Mortgage Reform and Anti-Predatory Lending Act, and other regulatory bills were introduced by both federal and state legislators. The regulations found in these bills tightened lending standards, with financial institutions now limited on how much risk they can take when it comes to the credit worthiness of a borrower, as well as the type of investments deemed appropriate for a bank. The result of these regulations was that banks simply stopped dealing with anyone but prime borrowers. Non-conventional lenders were more than willing to step in and help meet the demand from borrowers who sat just below the prime level. Because regulations focused on owner-occupied housing, non-conventional lending turned its focus to commercial or business property loans to avoid falling under federal guidelines. These borrowers were significantly more likely to repay loans than the borrowers private lenders had been dealing with prior to the financial crisis.

Historically Low Interest Rate Environment

A zero-interest-rate environment popped up as the Federal Reserve tried to deal with the recession by artificially holding down the target federal funds rate—the rate banks pay each other for overnight lending, or *floats*—to encourage the movement of capital within the financial system, as well as pumping funds into the markets by buying massive amounts of bonds. Lowering the interest rate for interbank movement is one of the weapons in the Federal Reserve's arsenal in dealing with recessions, because it results in lowering consumer interest rates, as well as fixed-income bond rates. These low interest rates not only prompted investors to pile into the rehab boom but also had them looking around for better fixed-rate returns than they could get from their standard bond investments. This benefited the private loan industry from both borrower and lender perspectives. Rehabbers were in the market for the short-term, no-hassle loans found in the private market, while high-net-worth investors and family offices were more than willing to lend to them to achieve the relatively high fixed-income returns found in the sector.

TODAY'S ENVIRONMENT

Today, the non-conventional lending industry is finding itself in something of a paradox. The success of private lenders during the past ten years has resulted in a significant jump in the number of investors wanting to take part in the sector. At the same time, the number of good rehab properties needing private loans—the real bread and butter for the industry—is decreasing. The rehab boom, which had been the foundation for much of the recent lending, is starting to revert to normal, because the inventory created after the crash has largely been exhausted. However, as of the writing of this book, banks are still heavily regulated and restricted as to whom they can lend to, and prime interest rates have continued to hover in the 1 percent to 2 percent range. This has resulted in an increasing amount of capital chasing a decreasing amount of inventory as investors seek to increase their fixed-income returns. Private lenders are seeing their lending risk rise without a concurrent rise in returns, though I would argue the benefits still far outweigh the risks.

Throughout this review of the evolution of lending, from non-conventional lending through the growth of institutional lending and the reemergence of non-conventional lending, we have focused on the creditworthiness of the borrower. But with non-conventional lending, we should be placing just as much, if not more, of our emphasis elsewhere—specifically, on the value of the property that is securing the loan. This is what makes non-conventional loans much safer than most investors believe.

Although non-conventional loans can be made on anything, the industry today is primarily focused on commercial real estate and real-estate–related businesses, such as the flippers we've all seen on TV. Unlike mortgages focused on owner-occupied residences, mortgages used for business purposes are a less regulated part of the investment world and thus are a sector with excellent returns that private investors can more easily access.

LOOKING TO THE FUTURE

Non-conventional lending has obviously been around for a long time, yet relatively few investors know about its benefits. Part of this has to do with the fact that conventional investors are only now beginning to routinely add alternative investments to their portfolios. Real estate is the first alternative to reach the almost-mainstream level.

But a lot of the lack of interest comes from simply not knowing about the sector. It is still an extremely opaque and fragmented market. There is no central clearinghouse, no central exchange, nowhere for investors and borrowers to find each other, nowhere to find a comprehensive list of choices, and nowhere to compare lenders and borrowers to make sure they are legitimate. It is still very much a word-of-mouth industry, and if you are not in the know, you are not going to have many choices.

Going forward, we need to find ways to shine a light on the industry so more can participate. We need more transparency and more standardization so borrowers can know what to expect and investors can know what they need to know. We need more information on what investors taking on specific risk levels should expect to receive in return.

As a private enterprise, everyone would still be able to make whatever deals they like—they'll just know they are deviating from the standard, rather than going in blind. As more non-conventional investors become familiar with the industry and begin to take part, there will undoubtedly be changes that make it more transparent and investor-friendly.

How can we shine that light? It all starts with educating people on this space.

KEY TAKEAWAYS FROM CHAPTER 2:

1. Non-conventional lending has been around for millennia and predates banking.

2. There have been several crashes over time, and there seem to be approximately seventeen years between each crash.

3. Non-conventional lending is still very much based on word of mouth, and it's time to standardize it.

TAKE ACTION *NOW*

Go to http://www.nonconlendingguide.com/Chapter2 for updated information, resources, and secrets.

KEY QUESTION:

On a scale of 1–10, how comfortable are you directing your own investments?

CHAPTER 3

NON-CONVENTIONAL LENDING EXPLAINED

Back in 2009, right after the subprime crash, I was doing a lot of the loan documents for a client who was making non-conventional loans. One day he said, "Hey, do you ever want to invest in this stuff?" I sort of brushed him off. Our team was focused on transforming my law firm from its traditional law firm structure into a more efficient corporate structure, and I wasn't sure I had the time or knowledge to jump into something new. But then, a few months later, he brought me a deal that was straightforward. I felt I could understand the underwriting, as well as the risks and rewards. Now, it is at this point that novice investors often get into trouble, because they don't know what they don't know, such as the true value of the property, the level of reliance on appraisers and brokers, how to confirm that the borrower is able to execute the proposed business plan, and other risks, but I knew and trusted this client, so I decided to jump in.

The borrower was looking for a second trust deed to finish a rehab project. The first trust deed was 60 percent LTV. Back in 2009, no financing source was going to make a second trust deed—not even non-conventional lenders. Because she would lose everything without that loan, I could name my price. I ended up loaning her $20,000 at 20 percent and getting paid back in just three months. The borrower was happy because she needed the money to finish the project. I was happy because of the rate of return, as was the broker.

Having done one deal, I quickly rolled the payoff into another investment, which was equally as profitable. It was another loan to the same borrower, except this time she needed $30,000, and again I got paid 20 percent on my money (not annually) in three months. It wasn't long before I decided that this was a pretty good way to invest. I had more control than I had when investing in stocks. I received a much higher return than when investing in bonds. Admittedly, I had to put in a little more work during the due diligence phase, and there have been properties that I have had to take over, but the returns are well worth it. In addition, taking control of the property is not necessarily a bad thing. Adding real estate to your portfolio is one of the easiest ways to boost returns while decreasing the overall portfolio volatility inherent in stocks.

THE BASICS

Have you ever purchased a home? Did you pay all cash for it? Maybe you can now, but I bet you didn't when you bought your first house. Even if you could pay cash, maybe there are reasons not to. Mark Zuckerberg, founder of Facebook, could easily have paid cash for his home, but he opted for a mortgage because he could get it at a 1 percent interest rate. Factor inflation in, and the bank lost money by lending to Zuckerberg—or did it?[18]

Mark Zuckerberg had a valid reason to borrow money to buy a house, and lots of other buyers do, as well. Those who qualify for a traditional bank-backed mortgage usually go that route. But there are others who might not qualify for a bank loan, or maybe they have reasons to look elsewhere. This is where the non-conventional lender enters the picture. As the person with the capital, the lender can choose whom he or she wants to lend money to, and on what terms. Given the amount of returns the lender can realize and the amount of money changing hands, it's a simpler transaction than you might imagine.

THE THREE COMPONENTS OF NON-CONVENTIONAL LENDING

At its core, being a non-conventional lender is very much like being a bank. Both sources of capital revolve around the same three main components: (1) a promissory note, (2) a security instrument, and (3) the property. Let's discuss these in detail.

- Promissory note—The promissory note is the promise—I promise to pay you, the lender, back with interest through agreed-upon payments, typically monthly. But you don't just accept the borrower's promise to pay you—this isn't a loan

---

18 It didn't. After all, from the bank's point of view, it is just lending on deposits. With Zuckerberg's net worth in the billions, the bank had virtually no risk, and the bank was paying less than 1 percent to depositors. Thus, it made money by arbitrage. You and I don't have that option. The house always wins.

to your sister, where she promises to pay you back and never does. No, you want to make sure you get paid back. Thus, you want your loan secured by the property the borrower is willing to put up as collateral to secure your loan. What secures the property? Answer: the security instrument!

- Security instrument—Depending on your state, the security instrument is a deed of trust, a mortgage, or, if you live in the state of Georgia, a security deed. In short, the security instrument promises that the lender gets to sell the property if the borrower does not make his or her payments in the manner promised.

- Property—The property is what is actually being secured. It will be what will be foreclosed on should the borrower not pay you.

A TYPICAL NON-CONVENTIONAL LENDING TRANSACTION

Every transaction is different, but all have a common starting point—the lender and borrower have to find each other. As mentioned earlier in the book, this is a very opaque industry with no central clearinghouse to help participants connect. Instead, the industry relies on word-of-mouth, primarily through brokers and attorneys who deal with the types of properties and borrowers often in need of private lending. If you want to become a private lender, referrals are essential. That means you need to spend some time finding the brokers and attorneys in your area who are familiar with non-conventional lending and let them know you are interested. Let them know the type of borrower you are looking for, and they'll let you know if they have someone who matches your requirements.

Once you have connected with a borrower, you'll need to do your due diligence. Because it is so important, we'll cover this topic in more detail later, but for now, you need to know that you have two areas to explore—the property and the borrower. The property will secure the loan, so you need to do the same level of due diligence that you would if you were buying it—because if things go wrong, you might be. You'll want to do all the inspections and crunch the comps to make sure you know its true value. The bottom line on property underwriting is asking the question: If I had to take over the property, could I sell it for a price that would cover my loan?

Focusing on the property doesn't mean that you ignore the borrower. You'll want to check borrowers' credit history, ability to repay the loan, ability to execute their business plan, and what sort of Plan B they have if Plan A doesn't work out. Because this is a non-conventional loan, you have the flexibility to look past some glitches in credit history or employment record that a bank can't. What you shouldn't look past is the borrower's character. You will want to make sure they are someone you want to do business with. Are they trustworthy? Will they do the right thing if faced with a choice that could go either way? If the property itself is a good investment, you can usually take a chance on a borrower that the bank would not—as long as the borrower is someone you want to take that chance on.

THE ART OF THE DEAL

If your due diligence has shown that the property is a good investment, and the borrower is worth backing, then it is time to move on to the terms of the deal. This is a non-standardized industry, so everything is negotiable. Items you'll want to cover in the terms include the following:

Length of loan. When is the final payment due? Can the loan be extended? What would be required for an extension?

Frequency of payments. Do you want monthly payments? Lump sum payment at end of loan? Interest-only during duration of loan, with lump sum principal repayment at end?

Default. If payments aren't made, what is your recourse? What steps need to be taken to declare the loan in default?

Yield. Yields (you've been waiting for this one) vary based on a number of factors, but non-conventional transactions can yield anywhere from 6 percent to 18 percent. Typically, investors can expect somewhere in the 8 percent to 12 percent range. What goes into determining your yield? Quite a few things.

- **Market conditions**—Probably the greatest consideration of your yield is market conditions—what is your friendly competitor private lender offering for a similar loan? In areas with lots of private lending competition for good properties, the interest rates are going to be lower than in an area where the borrower has fewer choices.

- **Loan-to-value**—What is the LTV percentage? The lower the LTV, the lower the yield a borrower will likely agree to.

- **Lien position**—Is it a first mortgage, or a second? You will get a higher yield or return on a second mortgage, because it is less secure than a first.

Implied risk. The most subjective element of the deal is placing a value on the implied risk of the property. This risk category covers all other intangibles, including likelihood of the borrower to default, the possibility of the property value decreasing, changing zoning codes, and other risks that can affect the ability of the borrower to repay the loan.

THE BENEFITS OF NON-CONVENTIONAL LENDING

Typical returns of 8 percent to 12 percent—with some being as low as 6 percent and others reaching 18 percent or even higher—are certainly the main benefit for investors, yet lending on real estate provides a much broader benefit in diversifying your portfolio, as well as reducing some of the risk introduced by relying on a volatile stock market for higher-than-fixed-income returns.

Real Estate Boosts Portfolio Returns

Institutional investors—pension funds, insurance companies, foundations, endowments, sovereign wealth funds, and some very large family offices—have long recognized the advantages of investing in real estate. More than two decades ago, Roger Ibbotson and his team produced groundbreaking research that showed adding private real estate to a diversified portfolio of stocks and bonds not only decreased volatility (risk) but also increased returns.[19] Since then, institutions have increased their real estate allocation to about 10 percent of their portfolio to access the sector's diversification, income, and appreciation benefits. Real estate is seen as so beneficial to the performance of a portfolio that many of the top-tier managers in the real assets world argue it should be at least 25 percent of the total portfolio.

---

19   "The Impact of a Real Estate Allocation in a Diversified Portfolio", Lazard, http://
www.lazardnet.com/us/docs/sp0/11291/TheImpactOfARealEstateAllocationInA.
pdf?pagename=Financial+Advisors; "Ibbotson update finds REITs improve
portfolio performance over time," Nareit, https://www.reit.com/sites/default/
files/media/Portals/0/Files/Nareit/htdocs/newsroom/ibbotson2002.pdf.

Unfortunately for most private alternative investors, real estate is simply out of reach. It can be too expensive and involve too much property management. In addition, it can be hard to get out of if you need the capital for something else. Anyone putting equity into real estate needs to be looking for a long-term investment.

But participating on the debt side of real estate deals is much more approachable. In fact, the institutional world is moving to the debt side as it looks ahead to the slowing of real estate equity returns. Real estate is a cyclical asset class tied to GDP. The US economic growth that started in 2009 is now the third-longest expansion in the country's history. During this period, real estate has done nothing but increase in value. Professional investment managers are looking at pricing, supply, and demand and saying this might be the time to take a slightly more defensive stance. Debt is considered defensive, because those holding the debt on a property get their investment back before those holding the equity.

The capital stack below illustrates this concept. The lower on the stack, the more secure the investment.

CAPITAL STACK

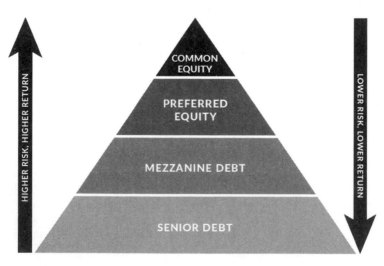

Non-conventional lending has the advantage of sitting in the safer debt section of the stack while typically realizing higher returns than traditional senior debt or mezzanine loans.

HIGH YIELDS IN ANY WORLD

The interest rates on ten-year treasuries, the most liquid and most widely traded fixed-income instrument in the world, remained stubbornly low after the GFC. As the Fed engaged in quantitative easing—buying massive amounts of bonds to pump capital into the frozen financial system—rates were kept unnaturally low. Even as the government began to unwind the quantitative easing—selling the bonds it was holding in its portfolio on the open market—it did it very slowly, and rates rose even more slowly. At the end of 2017— ten years after the beginning of the financial crisis—rates were still hovering around 2.4 percent. One-year treasuries were returning just 1.3 percent.

Returns in the 2 percent to 3 percent range were historically low, but even average returns aren't anything to write home about— or rely on for your retirement income. For example, the historical average yield for ten-year treasuries is just 6.24 percent.[20] Six percent would be the low end of the yield range for non-conventional loans (where you would also expect low LTV ratios). The average yield is several percentage points higher.

Non-conventional lending solves this low-rate return problem. With returns averaging 8 percent to 12 percent and often going higher, investors can double, triple, or even quintuple their investment returns while staying in the fixed-income portion of the capital stack.

---

20   US Department of the Treasury, YCharts, https://ycharts.com/indicators/ 10_year_treasury_rate

In addition, you get paid interest on the entire loan, even if you have not disbursed it all. When providing capital for a rehab project, for example, it is standard practice to disburse the loan in installments as the rehab progresses. This protects the lender from losing money if the borrower is unable to complete the project.

For example, Bill wants to borrow $200,000 at 8 percent interest to purchase a house to rehab. He needs $125,000 for the purchase and an additional $75,000 for the renovation costs. The lender would likely initially provide the $125,000 for the purchase and $25,000 to begin the rehab. As certain milestones are hit—HVAC system replaced, kitchen renovated, roof repaired, landscaping completed, etc.—the lender would provide another installment. The lender, however, gets paid interest on the entire loan amount from day one.

SECURED BY HARD ASSETS

Unlike loans based solely on a borrower's credit score, non-conventional lending on real estate looks primarily (but not solely) at the hard, immovable asset (the property) that the lender can take over and sell if necessary. Although it is certainly easier and less messy if the borrower simply repays the loan with interest, as agreed, I've often made more on houses I had to repossess and sell than I would have on the paid-off loan. So, while no one likes to foreclose on a loan in default, having a loan secured by a hard asset is a very real advantage to the investor.

INVESTOR CAN SET TERMS

You, as the non-conventional investor, are the one with the money; therefore, you get to set the terms. The terms are generally only limited by what the market is offering, as well as what the borrower will agree to. You might not be able to get a borrower to agree to 15 percent interest if someone else is willing to make the loan at 12 percent. You might want a three-month loan when the borrower needs six months to finish the project. Remember, all terms are negotiable, and there are more people who need capital for their projects than there are people able to lend capital. If you can't come to terms with one borrower, move on to another.

SECURE, HIGH-RATE INCOME STREAM

Investors have always turned to real estate for its secure, regular cash flow. Whether you are a retiree looking to boost your monthly income or a millennial just starting out and looking to boost your investment returns, private lending provides a secure cash income stream. It is very similar to other fixed-income investments, only better.

BALANCING THE EQUATION

Although the lender usually controls the transaction terms by being the one with the cash, it is important to remember that non-conventional lending is equally beneficial to the borrower. Primary advantages include the following:

- **Flexible, personalized terms**—Individuals seeking financing from a non-conventional lender often have unique needs. Maybe they want to forego payments for the first sixty days to help with cash flow at the beginning of the project. Maybe they want some sort of adjustable interest rate. Maybe they want the option to extend the loan for an additional three months with no penalty. Whatever they need, they can't get it from a bank, because banks have processes that they can't deviate from. A non-conventional lender can have the flexibility that nontraditional borrowers need.

- **Credit requirements less stringent than those required by bank loans**—Self-employed borrowers often find it difficult to qualify for bank financing. Because a non-conventional lender is not tied to strict credit metrics, a self-employed house flipper will typically find a much warmer welcome at the office of a non-conventional lender than that of their neighborhood banker.

- **Fast, efficient turnaround**—Private lenders are often loaning money from their own accounts, so there is no downtime once the paperwork has been signed. This is an advantage to borrowers who need to get working on their projects immediately or need to provide the cash to close a deal.

- **Loan sizes geared to fit the situation**—There are no maximum or minimum loan sizes, so a rehabber who just needs an additional $10,000 can find a lender as easily as someone looking for several hundred thousand.

- **Unusual property types are no problem**—Many alternative real estate classes are becoming popular with investors. These include rental units, self-storage properties, and mixed-use assets. While these are great income properties, traditional banks typically will not finance them. For the borrower looking to buy and/or rehab one of these properties, the non-conventional lending market is the place to be.

Being able to use someone else's money to buy and renovate properties gives rehabbers and other real estate investors the ability to turn properties quicker and renovate more properties at once than they would if they had to wait for the sale of each property before buying another. What they pay in interest to you, they make up in volume. In addition, sellers love cash buyers, so the borrower will often get a better price for the property if he or she can present an all-cash offer (based on your cash) along with a quick closing (because you don't need to deal with all the paperwork a bank does).

This is very much a symbiotic relationship. Active lenders and borrowers often develop long-term relationships, as they grow to trust each other. Those who can't be trusted soon find themselves with no one to borrow from or lend to, depending on the side of the equation they are coming from.

LENDER/BORROWER RISKS TO BE AWARE OF

When investing, you get paid for the risk you take. That is why AAA bonds return a lot less than BBB bonds. It's also why a non-conventional lender is going to be able to demand a higher interest rate than a bank. But if you do the proper due diligence, you can mitigate much of the risk found in providing capital to a third party. Some things to consider before getting into the private lending business include the following:

- **Market knowledge**—Your security is going to be the property and your ability to sell it if necessary. That means you need to know the market well enough to determine its value. I was an experienced lender when I made the mistake of lending on a property in an area I was unfamiliar with. When the borrower defaulted, I took possession of the property with the intent to quickly sell at what I thought was a below-market rate, but still well above what I needed to cover the loan. It turned out the demographics of the town and prospective buyers skewed heavily toward first-, second-, and third-generation Chinese Americans, and unfortunately, the house was not feng shui compliant.

  Feng shui is an ancient Chinese tradition that encompasses a set of beliefs and guidelines around energy flow—how to encourage good energy and spirits while discouraging bad energy and evil spirits. According to feng shui principles, energy flow is affected by the spatial arrangement and orientation of rooms and houses. A staircase might block good energy, or a misplaced window might allow bad energy to enter and be trapped inside. A hallway straight from the front door to a back slider allows good energy to enter and leave without stopping to visit. That's less than ideal. In China, feng shui principles are nearly always taken into account when designing buildings and arranging furniture.

At the time, I had never heard of feng shui (I know all about it now) and how important its principles are to those who adhere to them. I had to keep dropping my price to finally find someone who didn't care that the staircase faced the front door. It's that type of knowledge that makes getting to know local brokers so important. Nothing beats learning the quirks of a neighborhood from someone who lives and works there.

- **Liquidity**—When making private loans, you need to assume you will not get your money back when promised. In reality, borrowers almost always hold up their side of the contract, but you have to prepare for those who don't. If you can't afford to lose some of your principal or have it returned several months later than expected, this is not the investment for you.

- **Additional costs**—It is not unusual for the borrower to need additional capital before the project is completed. We've all seen the flipper shows where they *always* find that the HVAC system needs to be replaced or the garage was unpermitted, and rectifying the situation is going to take another $15,000. While you are under no obligation to supply this funding, it is often better to loan the additional capital than to see the project left unfinished. Therefore, prudent lenders will keep a certain amount of capital in reserve in case they are asked to cover an unexpected expense (though why are they unexpected when they always pop up?).

- **Valuations**—Valuing the property correctly is crucial. If you overvalue the asset, you risk loaning too much and not being able to recover your principal if the borrower defaults. For example, you might be willing to loan 80 percent of a property's value. If you appraise the property at $200,000, this means you are putting $160,000 in. If it turns out, however, that the property is only worth $150,000 by the time you want to sell—remember how fast values fell in 2007?—you will be losing money. A prudent way to value properties is to get several appraisals and then subtract 10 percent from the average. From that figure, only lend up to 65 percent to 75 percent of that value. This should offer very adequate protection, though nothing is foolproof. Overvaluing property was the downfall of the majority of brokers and banks during the housing crisis. You do not want to be part of that.

- **Insurance and paperwork**—You need to protect your right to the property, so be sure to get title insurance in case you missed something during your due diligence. You want to make sure it protects your rights as a lien holder. This insurance should protect you against fraud and forgery, as well. This is a business proposition. Treat it like one, even if you are lending to your grandmother. You do not want to find out when you or the borrower goes to sell the property and pay off the loan that you don't have clean title. You will also want to make sure you are listed on the borrower's property insurance policy as the lienholder. You want the insurance company to send you your money first if the house burns down or slides down a hill during an earthquake.

- **Regulations**—Every city, county, and state has its own regulations concerning property sales and financing. These can make the whole transaction much more complicated than it needs to be. The best way to mitigate the risk of running afoul of a restriction that you didn't know about is to have the appropriate disclosures and security documents drawn up by an experienced attorney. Look for one with specific experience in private lending. An additional benefit of using an experienced private lending attorney is that they will also be a good source for future borrowers, as attorneys who work for one lender or borrower generally work for several.

Any loan runs the risk of not being paid back, but non-conventional lending is not as risky as many would make it out to be. In my mind, the stock market is much riskier. With private lending, I am in control. I can make sure I thoroughly vet the property and the borrower to mitigate risks. If the borrower defaults, I have a hard asset that I can sell. No one will convince me that what I do is as risky as putting money into a stock market that can lose its value overnight. Real assets have an intrinsic value, so a prudent lender is very unlikely to lose his or her entire investment.

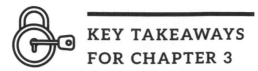

KEY TAKEAWAYS
FOR CHAPTER 3

1. The three components to a loan:

   a. Promissory note—this is the actual debt instrument the borrower signs. Don't' lose it!

   b. Security instrument—this is the document that secures the debt on the real property in question. This should be recorded in the county the property is located in.

   c. Property—the security for the debt. If you underwrote it correctly, you should have plenty of equity in it!

2. Typical returns are 8 percent and above in non-conventional lending for first liens and 12 percent and above for second liens.

3. With any return there is a risk, and the non-conventional investor has a few:

   a. Underwriting—get it right! It's the core of what you have to do!

   b. Regulatory—make sure you have a good attorney to advise you on the numerous laws that could come back to haunt you.

   c. Market—everything bears a market risk. If you're counting on 8 percent, then you'll need to either shift your risk by looking at riskier loans (higher LTVs, different property types) or look outside your state/country for returns of that nature. If your state gets overheated with non-conventional loans, all things being equal, your risk will have to increase.

TAKE ACTION *NOW*

1. Do you understand what a promissory note is? Check out http://www.nonconlendingguide.com for more information on this.

2. Review the investor videos on http://www.nonconexchange. com. These will help you get immersed in the non-conventional lending world.

GO here for updated information, resources, and secrets:

http://www.nonconlendingguide.com/chapter3.

Go to http://www.nonconexchange.com—the world's first non-conventional lending community exchange—to learn, connect, and grow!

KEY QUESTION:

How can non-conventional lending help you with your monetary and retirement goals?

CHAPTER 4

THE DIFFERENT FLAVORS OF LOANS AND BORROWERS

Non-conventional lenders have earned a not entirely unmerited reputation of sometimes being con artists. Lenders tell stories of the loans that went bad because the borrowers were untrustworthy at best, criminals at worst. And borrowers counter with stories of lenders whose primary motivation was acquiring the underlying property at a fraction of its real worth.

Those types of lenders and borrowers exist, but they are an extremely small minority in a growing and maturing industry that is filling a very necessary role in real estate financing. You can find a few bad apples in every industry, as well as law and government. Today, non-conventional lending has become a well-established source of financing that is meeting a need the banks can't meet and plays an important role in the growth of local economies. When bank financing dries up, as it did during the financial crisis, economic growth is throttled. It becomes a vicious cycle. Without financing, there is no growth. Yet without growth, there is no financing, because lenders need to know that future economic conditions will allow the borrower to pay off the loan. In addition, growth is needed to ensure that the flow of capital through the economic system continues unimpaired. Without growth, local or one-off hiccups can cause the whole system to grind to a stop. With growth, these small hiccups are smoothed and don't cause a problem.

Non-conventional lenders broke through this stalemate by providing the financing needed to help clear the foreclosed and abandoned real estate from bank books and free up capital for the banks to begin lending again. It continued to help by providing financing to those who no longer qualified for bank loans simply because the recession had knocked them off their feet, thus allowing entrepreneurs and small businesses to recover much faster than they would have without the help of non-conventional lending.

Non-conventional lending has also provided a solution for investors who want to keep much of their portfolio in cash-flowing, fixed-income products (as is recommended by nearly all financial advisers) but need more than the 1 percent or 2 percent return they were getting after the crisis, even on long-term bonds, such as ten-year treasuries. To get an attractive return, investors found themselves considering even longer-termed instruments, such as the 100-year bonds being issued by countries such as Argentina, Spain, and Ireland. Despite coming out of bankruptcy just a year earlier, Argentina promised 7.9 percent yields.[21]

---

21   "How did Argentina pull off a 100-year bond sale?", *Financial Times*, https://www.ft.com/content/5ac33abc-551b-11e7-9fed-c19e2700005f

It was this historically low interest rate environment after the crisis—with few realistic alternatives for the reasonable investor—that really gave non-conventional lending the boost it needed to reach mainstream investors. When 100-year bonds issued by countries with troubled economies are finding buyers, you know there has to be something better out there.

That "something better" is non-conventional lending, which has now reached a level of maturity to begin dividing into specialties. Each specialty within the sector carries its own pros and cons. This means investors who seek to become lenders have a variety of risk/return profiles to choose from, and the borrowers who want to access this financing have more choice on terms than they've ever had before.

LENDERS FOR EVERY NEED

Non-conventional lenders can be broken into a variety of camps. They were originally termed *hard money lenders* due to the fact that lenders would lend their hard-earned money (or more accurately, their investors' hard-earned money) to borrowers. After the financial crisis, this term seemed to become synonymous with subprime lending, which was done by Wall Street tycoons through the issuance of pooled loans and sold to investors with little knowledge of the market but who were assured these were rated AAA by Moody's and other highly regarded rating systems.

When I cofounded the country's largest hard money lending association in 2009, the other cofounders and I brainstormed to find a better name that lenders could easily identify with and that was more accurate of the industry in 2009, after the financial crisis. After consulting with the largest hard moneylenders in America, we coined the phrase *private money lender.*

This term fit until now. Today's market is much more sophisticated, with multiple ways for borrowers to access loans, from traditional lenders to crowdfunding. The *private money lender* name no longer fits. *Non-conventional lender* does. This term fits the robustness needed in alternative lending, as well as the speed and sophistication of the new lenders today.

Non-conventional lenders span a spectrum ranging from large, regulated firms to less regulated, individual investors. The large firms typically follow strict licensing guidelines. They will have specific criteria for what makes a qualified borrower, as well as listed interest rates and repayment terms. The property being used for collateral will need to meet a checklist of due diligence criteria. As these guidelines are predetermined, borrowers can usually find each lender's requirements listed on their website. These terms and criteria will be more lenient than those of a standard bank, but they are not typically negotiable. Large firms all have different loan products, as well. They could provide short-term financing to rehabbers all the way to first mortgages for businesses.

Smaller investors still need to be licensed—or work through a licensed broker—but they can be much more flexible than the large, national firms. What they are willing to lend on is pretty much only limited by available capital and the length of time the investor wants that capital deployed. The terms of these loans are pretty much whatever is agreed upon.

Although individual investors can be much more flexible than the larger firms, they often don't have the skill or knowledge to underwrite property adequately and thus might end up lending on assets that can't support the loan. Determining whether a borrower has the wherewithal to repay the loan takes more than just looking at a credit score. Private investors rarely have the experience to make this judgment.

Many private investors solve this lack-of-skill problem by supplying the capital that the hard moneylender or larger lender lends out. This allows the private investor access to a lucrative source of income while off-loading most of the risk to a licensed professional. It also gives the private investor a larger universe of borrowers to choose from. As mentioned in an earlier chapter, this is a very fragmented market, and one of its primary downsides is the inability of borrowers and lenders to find each other. Hard moneylenders will advertise and seek out borrowers, whom they will then qualify. Having a licensed, experienced partner to find the borrowers, qualify them, underwrite the property, and make sure all rules and regulations are followed is a great way for an individual to mitigate the risks of the sector. Because of that, it is how most private lenders access the market.

TYPES OF LOANS

Although non-conventional lenders are flexible enough to make just about any type of loan—as long as they follow the regulations and licensing some types of loans trigger—in reality, most lenders specialize. As the industry has grown and matured, it only makes sense for lenders to tap into efficiencies of scale (and efficiencies of knowledge) by focusing on what they know and do best.

Rehab Loans
A rehab loan is pretty much what it says on the box: a loan to cover the cost of rehabbing or renovating a property. These loans are made on

properties that are being upgraded for profit, not personal residences. These loans can cover the cost of the house, the cost of the rehab, the cost of the house plus rehab costs, or any permutation of the above. Because it is an alternative source, you can slice and dice the financing just about any way you like. In my career, I have seen just about every permutation of rehab loan structure, from mezzanine to joint venture to several varieties of profit split. These loans typically allow enough flexibility for the non-conventional lender to tap some of the capital stack the borrower intends to access by themselves. For example, you are sometimes able to negotiate profit-sharing with the rehab lender as they need your money and you need their expertise.

A very conservative (i.e., smart, in my opinion) lender will finance up to 65 percent of the property's value, though 75 percent can be justified in many cases. The trick is to decide whether that is based on pre-rehab value or on ARV. A loan of 75 percent to 80 percent of the purchase price could very well be conservative, given that the property is expected to be worth much more after repairs. Lending 75 percent to 80 percent of the estimated ARV would not be conservative or wise. You don't know if that ARV is going to be achieved, so you don't want to base your LTV ratio on it. Borrowers, of course, like loans that base their upper limit on ARV. Lenders, on the other hand, like loans based on current value. As with most things, the market in each geographic area will dictate the interest rate for the risk by the lender.

LTV BASIS MAKES HUGE DIFFERENCE
IN BORROWER OUTLAY

	80% LTV of $200,000 Purchase Price	80% LTV of $300,000 ARV
Purchase Price	$200,000	$200,000
Loan	− $160,000	− $240,000
Rehab Costs	+ $50,000	+ $50,000
Bill's Out-of-Pocket Costs	= $90,000	= $10,000

Let's look at numbers to see how the base value affects the loan amount. Let's say that Sheila is looking at an older house in a good neighborhood, where homes range from $200,000 to $350,000. The house is part of an estate sale, and it had the same owners for thirty years. They made sure the roof, the foundation, and the electric and plumbing systems were all well maintained, but they had not updated the house for today's buyers. The estate agents are looking for a quick sale and have listed the house for $200,000. Sheila does her due diligence and is convinced that with about $50,000 in rehab costs (to update the kitchen and baths, put in hardwood floors, take down a couple of walls to open the main floor, and redo all the landscaping to make the outside a beckoning oasis), she can sell the house for $300,000.

A lender who is willing to lend 75 percent to 80 percent (fairly common LTV percentages) of the before-rehab value—i.e., the purchase price—of $200,000 will be offering Sheila $150,000 to

$160,000. Sheila will need to come up with an additional $90,000 to cover the remaining purchase and rehab costs.

However, if Sheila finds a lender willing to base its financing on ARV, she will keep a lot more of her own dollars in her pocket, but this is a much riskier proposition to the lender. This lender will be offering 75 percent to 80 percent of $300,000, so Sheila will be able to finance $225,000 to $240,000. In this scenario, Sheila will only need to come up with $10,000 to $25,000 of her own capital to finish the project. Sheila now has the purchase price and $25,000 to $40,000 of "profit" in her pocket. If Sheila decides to just walk away from the property without fixing it up, the lender is left holding the bag on this property and will likely need to rehab it themselves in order to get the maximum expected value.

Now, this is a simplified example. Lenders often require that the borrower ante up a specific percentage of the price plus rehab costs, despite the fact that the lender could, in theory, cover more of the costs. And most lenders will dole out the rehab part of the loan in installments as the work progresses to avoid providing funding to a rehabber who is unable to complete the project. But you get the idea of why the appraisal base can make a significant difference to the lender and the borrower.

I like to loan up to 65 percent to 75 percent on the current value of the property, because you simply can't be sure of the ARV. Estimating what a home will be worth before any work is done, and at a time that could be several months in the future, is risky. Anything can, and often does, happen between the start of rehab and the completion. Maybe the seller runs into the feng shui conundrum I experienced, as noted in an earlier chapter, and can't sell for the expected price. (I now often refer to events that take me completely by surprise as a "feng shui moment.") I believe lending on the current value is the more prudent way to go and the best way to prevent losses, but many lenders are comfortable using ARV. What you decide to do is between you and your financial adviser.

Rehab loans have been a favorite for non-conventional lenders and borrowers since the recession. They can cover single-family and multifamily residences, as well as business locations. Because the properties can be easily underwritten, the loans usually have a quick turnaround—often less than a week. If you are a lender using your own bank account or a borrower with an established relationship with such a lender, the turnaround might be completed in hours. The length of the loan depends on the work being done, but they are typically three to six months, though some lenders and borrowers like to write the contract for twelve months with no prepayment penalty. This gives the borrower time to rehab and sell the property, if that is the exit strategy, or to find renters, stabilize, and refinance the property, if that is the final goal.

One caveat: If you write your loan for twelve months, make sure that there are clauses guaranteeing that the loan proceeds can be used only for the specific property being used as collateral. You don't want the borrower to roll the funds over into a new project with the idea that because they don't need to repay the loan for a year, they have the right to use the funds for that entire time.

Interest rates on rehab loans generally run about 5 percentage points higher than for a conventional loan for a specific property. This is to pay the lender for the extra risk inherent in these projects, as well as for the short time frame. When the loan is paid off, the lender will need to find another borrower to continue receiving interest on that capital. It's not unusual for the capital to sit idle while a lender and borrower try to find each other. These loans are almost always interest-only, with the principal paid off at the end, so monthly payments are reasonable despite the higher interest rate.

Make sure you consult with an attorney who specializes in non-conventional lending, as there are many clauses in your loan documents that should be included to protect you. And never, never, *never* use escrow-prepared loan documents. You're investing hundreds of thousands of dollars of your money in these loans; now is not the time to be cheap and worry about a couple of thousand dollars on loan documents that your borrower is going to pay for anyway.

Bridge Loans

Bridge loans are short-term loans used to get the borrower through a time-limited financial challenge. For example, Bill has a rehabbed house under contract. If all goes well at closing, he will clear about $40,000 after closing costs and paying off the rehab loan he took out three months earlier. Once the house closes, he expects to roll the profits into a new project. One day, he sees the perfect next project. It has a $300,000 price tag, but comps in the neighborhood are running over $400,000. He wants this house, but to make an offer he needs a 10 percent deposit, which he doesn't have at the moment. If he waits until his current project closes, he will likely lose out on the new one. He needs a loan to cover the deposit.

Traditional banks will not touch this type of loan, but it is perfect for a non-conventional lender. The source of the repayment capital is obvious and secure. The time frame is short, and the borrower is willing to pay a premium interest rate, because it is only for a few weeks. Non-conventional lenders would be falling all over each other to make this loan—if it was easier for borrowers and lenders to get together and Bill had access to multiple lenders. Finding a lender is usually the hardest part of the whole process, but Bill already has a relationship with the non-conventional lender who had financed the original rehab and will finance the next. So, instead of waiting for the first house to close, he goes back to his lender for a $30,000 bridge loan to cover the gap in financing.

Due to the fact that they have an established relationship, the non-conventional lender is able to process the loan within twenty-four hours, and Bill is able to make his bid. As soon as the first house closes, he will pay off the original rehab loan plus the new bridge loan and then take out a new rehab loan to fund his business.

Owner-Occupied Loans

Most non-conventional lenders will not make a loan on an owner-occupied property—e.g., a mortgage for a primary residence—because of the regulations covering those loans. Owner-occupied mortgages are some of the most regulated loans in the industry. It was the lack of discipline by traditional banks (surprise, surprise) surrounding these mortgages that arguably caused the financial crisis—or at least played a major role in it—and so, in seeking to prevent another meltdown, the government passed regulations to prevent the type of subprime lending prevalent in the early 2000s.

A couple of requirements found in these regulations are particularly troublesome for alternative lenders. First of all, lenders must use a third-party verification source to ensure that the borrower has the ability to repay the loan. This source typically verifies income, as well as the borrower's ability to stay below a certain debt-to-income ratio. If the loan is a "high-cost loan"—a loan where the annual percentage rate (APR) and/or points and fees come in higher than a regulated threshold—additional requirements kick in, including a requirement that the lender hold the property taxes and insurance premiums in escrow for at least the first year and be responsible for making those payments.

Because most non-conventional lenders are not set up to meet all the requirements found in the Truth in Lending Act, Regulations X and Z, the Home Ownership and Equity Protection Act, and the Real Estate Settlement Procedures Act (to name just the most common and well-known regulations), they simply avoid these loans. Others have the back-office capacity to offer owner-occupied loans but prefer not to become involved, because it is too much of a hassle.

Lenders who do make owner-occupied loans often do so only if the funds are being used for a business purpose rather than buying the house. A business purpose could include creating a new business, investing in a business, or even remodeling an investment property. Loans used for business purposes do not fall under the newer home mortgage regulations, even if the collateral being used is a personal residence. These can be tricky, however, so consult with an attorney who specializes in non-conventional lending.

However, I believe that owner-occupied loans have a bright future for those willing to go through the regulatory hurdles. The simple fact is that if it was easy, everyone would be doing it. And since it's not, there's a market to get low-LTV loans at great ROIs as a result.

Consumer Loans

We've all made noninvestment consumer loans. Maybe we loaned a friend the first and last months' rent for an apartment. Maybe we loaned a brother or sister money to pay for their college tuition. Maybe we loaned our kid the down payment for a car—or maybe all of the above. These are the loans of everyday stuff, and they generally don't include an interest rate. In the industry, they call these gifts, because you're likely not going to get your money back! However, investment consumer loans are very different, because they are very regulated and will make you money.

Consumer loans are loans for family, personal, or household use. Some of the more common uses of consumer loans are bill consolidation, paying off taxes or liens, buying a car, or covering school tuition. Non-conventional lenders do not often lend to this group, because the regulations to do so are tight, but anyone willing and able to meet the consumer protection regulations will find these loans lucrative, as the interest rates can be very attractive.

Consumer loans generally fall into two categories: (1) bridge loans for personal residences, and (2) longer-term personal, family, or household loans.

Consumer bridge loans are often used by borrowers who need just a bit of time to rectify things that banks don't like. For example, a borrower might not have a long enough employment history to qualify for a conventional loan. A bridge loan might allow them to purchase a house now, rather than next year. By the time the consumer bridge loan is coming to an end, the borrower should be able to refinance with a traditional mortgage provider.

Other common situations include divorces, where one of the spouses needs to purchase a house before the divorce settlement is finalized or needs a loan to buy the other spouse out of the property; a glitch on the credit history that will fall off in the next few months; and help with the down payment for a borrower who is using a traditional loan to cover the mortgage but is waiting for some other source of capital to clear for the down payment.

Some lenders prefer to make long-term loans (i.e., loans longer than a year), because they like the longer guaranteed income. Borrowers seeking longer-term loans usually have credit or employment problems that need to be worked out, or "seasoned," before a traditional lender will look at them. Consumer regulations state how these loans are amortized and provide other protections for the borrower that the lender needs to be aware of.

The downside of consumer bridge loans is the risk that a consumer who does not qualify for a traditional loan may not be a good candidate for a non-conventional loan either. Although real estate is still usually the collateral on the loan, you will be in a second-lien position, as the first-position mortgage will be the lien that the borrower purchased the home with. This means that if things go south, you will have to either decide to foreclose on the borrower, if there will be enough for you, or decide whether to pursue the borrower just on the basis of the note. Great advice on this issue can be found on http://www.nonconexchange.com.

BORROWERS FOR EVERY LENDER

Just as lenders span a spectrum from conservative to opportunistic and from rigid to flexible, borrowers also come in all shapes and sizes.

I like to call the borrowers I work with "entrepreneurs." They tend to be self-employed rehabbers who make their living by finding good real estate that can be renovated and sold for a profit. These are business people who know what they are doing, have an executable business plan, and have a record of successfully executing that plan and paying off the loan on time. I have also provided financing for entrepreneurs who buy both single-family and multifamily residences to renovate and hold for rental.

These are creditworthy individuals with realistic real estate development plans, but banks won't touch them. Being self-employed is one problem; banks want to see steady, W-2 income from a stable source. The time frame is a problem; banks like longer-term financing. The property is a problem; banks don't like dilapidated properties, because they are hard to assess. But all of the things banks dislike, I and other non-conventional lenders find attractive.

Every professional rehabber had to have a first-time project, and I've financed my share of those. Because first-time and one-time flippers don't have a track record, you need to be extra careful and conservative. Check that the entrepreneur has the skills required to do the work. Make sure the house value will cover the loan and then some. Pay close attention to the borrower's ability to repay. Because first-timers are considered riskier, you can charge a higher interest rate to pay for the risk you are taking. If you have the risk tolerance to finance first-timers, it can be very profitable and can help someone get started on a new career path.

Other types of borrowers are mentioned earlier: the entrepreneur who needs a bridge loan, because he finds his second project closing before the sale of his first; or the home buyer who needs a consumer loan to cover a down payment until she qualifies for other financing. There are probably as many types of borrowers as there are things to buy. As long as they have a house that can be used for collateral, they can be part of the growing universe of non-conventional lending participants.

KEY TAKEAWAYS FROM CHAPTER 4:

1. Non-conventional lenders have moved from generalizing their lending business to specializing in certain types of loans.

2. There are several flavors of loans, but these are the basic categories:

a. Rehab loans—This is lending to a "fix and flipper," or a borrower who will rehabilitate a home.

b. Bridge loans—These are temporary loans that "bridge" the gap between the need for cash and the sale of the asset, or in the case of primary residences, bridge the gap between the borrower's old house and their new house.

c. Owner-occupied loans—These are loans secured by the borrower's primary residence, and they come in two flavors: business purpose and consumer purpose.

   i. Business purpose loans are generally exempt from most regulatory laws.

   ii. Consumer purpose loans are loans for personal, family, or household use and are some of the most regulated loans out there.

3. Understand (1) the borrower's motivation in getting the loan and (2) the collateral for the loan. From there you can determine whether this loan fits your investing portfolio.

TAKE ACTION *NOW*

1. Give some thought about what types of loans you want to invest in—business or consumer loans?

2. If you had to foreclose on the collateral, would you be okay with the loan you invested in?

3. Do you want a more passive investment? Consider investing in the Non-Conventional Lending Exchange's borrower-dependent notes or mortgage fund. See http://www.nonconexchange.com for more information.

Check out these websites for more information:

Originate Report—the non-conventional lender's origination re-source: http://www.originate.report

GeraciCon– conferences that teach you the ins and outs of the business: http://www.geracicon.com

http://www.nonconlendingguide.com/chapter4

http://www.nonconexchange.com

KEY QUESTION:

What are you most comfortable investing in or lending on in the non-conventional lending space?

CHAPTER 5

BECOMING PART OF THE NON-CONVENTIONAL LENDING WORLD

Now that I've explained what non-conventional lending is and how it can help you get better fixed-income returns while maintaining a lower risk profile than equities, we are finally getting to the heart of the matter: how you can be part of this world.

Becoming a non-conventional lender or investor is both easy and difficult. It's easy because, at its core, all you really need to do is have the capital to lend and a person to lend it to. It's hard because finding that person and understanding the intangibles, such as the character and credibility of a borrower, can be difficult.

Oftentimes I will work with new investors who seek to learn the business by calling me to discuss the non-conventional lending world.

After assessing their wants and needs, I will generally go through my contact list to connect them to one of our non-conventional lending clients who has deal flow. After advising them generally on the non-conventional lending space, we try to assist in analyzing the deal, the paperwork, and both consultative and legal advice, as it pertains to alternative lending.

When I first jumped into the non-conventional lending waters, I was lucky, because I had lived and breathed the world as the legal adviser for other lenders for quite some time. I understood the framework of the loan and had a built-in network of borrowers and lenders to tap for advice. So much of this industry is based on word of mouth.

But before we get to finding a network, there are questions you need to ask yourself to make sure you are prepared for this type of investment. I consider non-conventional lending less risky than equities, because returns are much less volatile than those derived from the stock market. Non-conventional lending is backed by a real asset with intrinsic value, so you can never lose 100 percent of your investment (as long as you hold the first-position mortgage). And determining the value of a property is easier to do than determining the true value of a company or predicting the movement of a stock that moves on rumors rather than company value. You could even make an argument (and I often do) that non-conventional lending is less risky than bonds, because the short-term nature of the loans protects you from interest rate risk (If interest rates continue to creep up over the next few quarters, what are those low-rate bonds in your portfolio going to be worth?) plus the interest you can charge truly pays you for the risk you are taking. I don't think other asset classes come close to paying for the true risk investors take, but that is probably a discussion for another book.

However, even though I find this investment sector to be the perfect place to put my capital, it is not right for everyone. Investors should qualify themselves for this investment sector by answering a series of questions.

Can I afford to make this loan?

With any investment, you need to be prepared to lose it (see the stock market from 2007–2009). However, given that the recourse if a borrower defaults on the loan is to take possession of the house and sell it, it is extremely unlikely that you will lose your principal. Lenders who do their due diligence on the property and make prudent loans never walk away with less than they put in. As the old saying goes, real estate has never been worth nothing!

Can I afford to wait for the loan to be paid off?

These are illiquid loans, so you should make sure you don't need the capital returned before it is due. The borrower can prepay, but you can't pre-call the loan (unless they don't pay you, of course, but fore-closure takes time). Lenders who need to liquidate their investment before the loan's maturity can sell the note on the secondary market, but they are likely to have to sell at a discount unless it is an excellent property with a creditworthy borrower, above-average interest rate, and timely payments. In addition, the borrower sometimes needs additional funds to finish a rehab, and you may well want to advance those funds to assure the project is completed. Other investors might need the loan to be extended a couple of more months for any number of reasons. While you can certainly refuse the extension, it often makes more sense to wait another ninety days to be paid off— usually with the borrower paying a penalty fee of some sort—than it does to foreclose.

The best ways to prevent stress in making these loans include (1) making sure you can afford to make the loan and having the savings and cash flow to cover your own expenses without this investment capital, (2) having a cushion of additional funds—maybe 10 percent—in case you need to add funds, and (3) having no need for the capital you are lending for the length of the loan plus an additional three months.

Do I have the time and skill to underwrite and service these loans?
Good news—you don't have to if you don't want to. A lot of non-conventional lenders like to do their own underwriting and servicing. They visit the property, inspect the foundation and roof, evaluate the neighborhood, and check comps and liens. They are hands-on and love it. But there are also firms that will provide all the heavy lifting. You can outsource just the underwriting and servicing, or you can invest with the firm and let them deal with the borrowers, as well. Check out our platform exchange at http://www.nonconexchange. com for both active and passive opportunities.

Am I prepared to take over the property,
finish the renovation, and sell it?
Again, this is all something you can outsource if you don't have the time, knowledge, or personality to do yourself. Foreclosing on a borrower can be unpleasant. Getting the property ready for sale can take more time than you want to give it. Many lenders have no problem with these tasks, but most use outside professionals, such as their legal advisers and alternative lending partners.

You should not go into the non-conventional lending business with the goal of getting your hands on a property at a fraction of its cost. Your goal should be to provide financing to someone with an executable business plan who will pay back the loan as promised and provide you with a cash-flowing, high-return investment. However, you need to be prepared to enforce the contract, and that sometimes means you will end up owning property, whether you want it or not. It's an option you need to be prepared for.

What is the average loan size? Is this something I am comfortable with?

The good news is there is no average (this asset class is full of good news, isn't it?). Some lenders stay in the $10,000 range, while others loan up to $10 million or more. Professional firms usually have limits on how much they will lend, but the reality is that you can finance as much or as little as you want to. It all depends on what the borrower needs and what you are able to invest. My first loan was only $20,000, so you don't need to have a huge amount of capital to take advantage of this opportunity.

What is the typical interest rate? Am I happy with the return I can make?

Interest rates vary depending on the competition, as well as the perceived risk. In general, these loans have an APR that ranges from 8 percent to about 14 percent—and on occasion, 6 percent or 18 percent—annually. I believe that those in the 6 percent range are a problem, as that rate is too close to traditional bank mortgage rates. Lenders making non-conventional loans at 6 percent are not being paid for the risk they are taking, nor for the time they put into underwriting and servicing the loan. There needs to be a much larger delta between non-conventional loans and traditional loans. I'd suggest that a 3 percent to 5 percent difference is a good ball park to play in.

*What is a typical repayment period? Is this
something I am comfortable with?*

Non-conventional loans generally span less than one year. Many are
in the three- to six-month range, though others, such as owner-occupied loans, can be long-term. The timing, like the loan amount, is
really negotiated by the lender and borrower. Payments are typically
made monthly and are usually interest-only throughout the life of
the loan. The principal is due at the end, presumably when the rehab
is completed and the house sold, or when the borrower is able to find
more traditional financing for his or her needs.

*How much of my diversified portfolio should
these loans typically account for?*

Most investors are comfortable having about 25 percent of their
portfolio in non-conventional loans. I personally think that these
loans should replace your entire fixed-income allocation. You will
realize significantly better returns at a lower risk level.

*I'm not sure I want to deal directly with the borrower. Is
there another way to invest in non-conventional loans?*

Absolutely. There are multiple ways to access this sector: (1) you can
access the non-conventional lending exchange at http://www.non-
conexchange.com, (2) you can invest in a pooled fund of loans, or
(3) you can find a broker who invests in this sector and would be
happy to invest your capital for you—for a fee, of course. Many non-
conventional lenders use capital from private investors such as you.
Currently, it is not easy to find the right fund or firm to work with,
but they are out there. Ask your local real estate brokers or mortgage
brokers, and check out sources like *Originate Report* (http://www.
originate.report), which is the industry's largest publication.

How do I structure non-conventional loans?

These loans are extremely flexible. Some lenders focus on just one area and become experts in a specific type of loan. Others mix and match, depending on their relationship with the borrower or broker. The following are a few of the more common type of loans that you can invest in:

- **First-position loans**—A first-position, first-lien, or first-mortgage loan is the main mortgage on a property. What it is used for—purchase, renovation, refinance, etc.—isn't as important as it being the first mortgage. Experienced lenders like these loans because they can control the terms. The downside of these loans is pretty much the same as the upside: You are dealing with one borrower and you are solely responsible to make things right if something goes wrong. However, if something does go wrong, you can foreclose, and assuming the due diligence was sound, your risk is minimal.

- **Second-position loans**—A second-position, second-lien, or junior loan captures higher returns than a first-mortgage loan, but the investor takes on substantially more risk to justify that higher return. Investors who hold a second lien can find themselves in a precarious position. For example, if the borrower is unable to keep up payments on the first mortgage, you might need to step in and pay off or bring current the first-position loan to protect your initial investment. In addition, falling market prices will affect second-position mortgages well before a first, meaning that you are much more likely to lose your investment in a declining market than you would be with a first mortgage in hand. Investors need to understand what they are getting into and remember that those higher rates come with higher risk.

- **Secondary-market transactions**—These are loans that have already been made, but the lender wants to sell the note and recoup his or her capital before the payoff date. The price you pay will vary by performance and length of time left on the loan. Some sell for face value. Some sell at a discount, particularly if they are nonperforming. If it is a particularly good loan, you might end up paying a premium. Lenders who invest in these types of loans like that they know exactly what they are getting. They can look at the borrower's payment history and be assured that monthly payments will continue through the life of the loan. If the loan is nonperforming but the property is solid and the discount is deep enough, lenders willing to foreclose or restructure the loan can end up with very attractive yields.

- **Loan pools**—If you want to smooth the risk, you can buy into a diversified group of loans. Buying a package composed of multiple originated loans means that even if one ends up defaulting, you still have others making their monthly payments, and your cash flow will be minimally affected. The downside is that you have to take all of the loans in the pool. Most will undoubtedly be good, performing investments, but there are likely to be a few dogs in the group as well.

- **Non-conventional mortgage funds**—Non-conventional mortgage funds are companies that pool investors' capital into commingled funds to make investments on behalf of the fund. Each investor owns part of the pool. These funds are managed by professional investment managers, and investors get the benefit of their skills and experience.

How do I find a credit-worthy entrepreneur in need of funding?
This is maybe the hardest part of all, because the industry is still so fragmented and opaque. You aren't going to find a list of experienced renovators or small businesses looking for financing on Google. Instead, you'll need to do a bit of phone calling and e-mailing.

Some of the best people to contact are local real estate and mortgage brokers. These are the people who often come in contact with professional flippers, small business owners, and others who need non-conventional loans, either because they are selling the property or because they have been approached for financing.

Real estate attorneys are another good source. These loans all need contracts and other legal documents generated to protect both lender and borrower. Law firms, such as mine, deal with both borrowers and lenders on a daily basis and are often willing to introduce borrowers and lenders to each other.

A less obvious source of borrowers is local Registered Investment Advisers (RIAs) who are familiar with this sector and recommend it to their clients. Because RIAs' income is contingent on providing advice that leads to successful investment outcomes, those who promote non-conventional loans for their clients are hyperaware of the good and bad actors out there.

How do I choose a broker/attorney/RIA to work with?
Do your homework. Start by looking at their track record. You want to work with someone experienced in the industry. A broker should have handled multiple properties and be willing to show you purchase

and sales records. An attorney should have handled the documentation for both borrowers and lenders and should be an expert in the non-conventional lending space. An RIA should be able to tell you how these investments have worked out for his or her clients (and be careful when they try to tell you, "Oh, those are too risky," and steer you into "safe" investments like stocks and bonds). A successful track record in the field is crucial, especially if you are new to the industry. You will be relying on these professionals to steer you in the right direction.

It would be rare for an experienced investor to have never been involved with a challenging borrower. Find out what kinds of contingencies he or she has in place to protect the investor's capital and what he or she has done in the past to rectify nonperforming loans.

While non-conventional lenders can and do loan directly with the borrower, most work through a broker, not only to find borrowers but also to provide the due diligence, legal advice, servicing, and other logistics involved in a property loan. If you are going to be relying on the broker for these services, be sure they are able to provide them, and know the cost.

Brokers and attorneys often specialize in specific types of loans and properties. Find one who has lots of experience in the area you want to jump into.

Ask to speak to other clients. Lenders who have worked with the broker in the past can vouch for his or her experience and business practices.

Finally, look for a broker who "clicks" with you. You and the broker are looking to be in this relationship for the long term. You want someone whom you feel has your best interests at heart and whom you feel confident will watch your capital the same way you would.

What do I need to know about the borrower?

You need to do due diligence on the borrower, but because the property is securing the loan, the borrower doesn't have to meet the exacting standards that a bank would require for the same type of loan. Check the borrower's credit score. You want someone who has the ability and desire to repay the loan. If you are making a regulated loan, you will need to dive a little deeper to make sure the borrower has the required income-to-debt ratio. But in the end, whom you deem a qualified borrower is pretty much up to you. Borrowers rejected by one lender are usually met with open arms by another.

What do I need to know about the property?

Everything. The property has one job: protect your capital. Therefore, you need to assure it can do that. Valuing the property correctly is the linchpin to everything else. If the property is appraised incorrectly, everything can come crashing down under stress. There are a couple of different ways to make it more likely that a property appraisal is accurate. You can have more than one appraisal done and compare the results. I would average the valuation, or even take the lower one, to make sure that I'm not overvaluing the property. I usually look at the professional appraisal and discount it by 10 percent to give myself a cushion if values go down, or if the appraiser just happened to be having a particularly optimistic day.

While it is crucial to have at least one formal appraisal done, nothing beats looking at the property yourself. While I have made loans on out-of-state properties that have turned out to be great investments, I much prefer driving out to a property and giving it a proper look. I drive around the neighborhood and get a feel for its character. Is it stable? Is it up-and-coming? Or does it look like it's on the way down?

I look at the location of the property. Does it back up to railroad tracks? Is the sun blocked by a towering manufacturing plant? Is it within walking distance to schools and retail? The appraiser is supposed to take these types of quality-of-life factors into consideration, but seeing the situation yourself adds data to what should be a data-driven decision.

You are also going to want to check out the condition and quality of the property. Assets that need cosmetic updates are usually safer investments than those that need a huge overhaul. More major projects, however, can provide higher yields. This is where the investor needs to decide how they want to lend capital. Lending to multiple, short-term, cosmetic updates can provide high yields but involves finding new properties every few weeks to reinvest the capital. Larger projects do not need to be churned, but they tie up your capital longer, so you might not be able to take advantage of other opportunities. Deciding which type of loan is best for you usually just comes down to whether you are looking for a make-it-and-forget-it investment (longer-term, major project investment) or a quick-in, quick-out investment where you'll take your chances on your capital being uncommitted for random periods of time (short-term, cosmetic projects).

If the property is too far away to check out in person, harness technology to help you. Google Maps has street views and pictures of houses, and get a local appraiser to appraise the property.

What are the tax implications to non-conventional lending?

This is one to take up with your tax adviser—and if you have the ability to make non-conventional loans, you should already have a tax adviser. However, in general, profits fall into the capital gains category, either short-term or long-term. Business expenses can be deducted, just as in any other business.

Is this the right time to invest in real estate debt?
I think any time is the right time to invest in real estate debt. The only thing that changes is the way you invest and where in the capital stack you want to be. I have a lot to say on this. In fact, I've written an entire chapter. Turn the page to see how to use non-conventional loans to realize above-average returns at any time in the market cycle.

KEY TAKEAWAYS FROM CHAPTER 5:

1. Real estate has never been worth nothing! Unlike stocks and bonds, where it's just someone saying a company is worth something, real estate is ... well ... real. You can touch it, see it, etc.

2. There are first liens, second liens, and even more junior liens. First liens are just that: first in line to be paid. Returns are lower, but risk is lower as well. Second liens are second to be paid and could be wiped out by the first lien but have higher returns.

3. Network with professionals in this space to get to know it as well as to establish deal flow. Also check out *Originate Report* (http://www.originate.report) and Non-Conventional Lending Exchange (http://www.nonconexchange.com) for networks of people to connect with.

TAKE ACTION *NOW*

1. Talk with your RIA, broker, and attorney to find out whether this kind of investment makes sense for you. But don't just take dogma as an answer—answer it yourself. Why wouldn't you want to invest in real estate as well as stocks and bonds?

2. If it is right for you, best practices show that 25 percent of your portfolio should be in non-conventional loans or non-conventional lending funds.

Check out these websites for more information:

http://www.nonconlendingguide.com/chapter5

Originate Report (to find brokers/lenders):
http://www.originate.report

Non-Conventional Lending Exchange:
http://www.nonconexchange.com

KEY QUESTION:

Are you interested in being active or passive in this space?

CHAPTER 6

INVESTING FOR TODAY'S (AND TOMORROW'S) ECONOMY

The majority of investors have a portfolio full of stocks and bonds—and little else. Sound familiar? I wouldn't be surprised if you just took a quick look at your investments or mentally ran down the list and realized that "stocks and bonds—and little else" pretty much describes your holdings. There is a very good reason for that.

For decades, financial advisers have focused on what they know. And what they know is stocks and bonds. They usually assure you that bonds for income and stocks for growth are all you need. They often talk about actively managing your portfolio by rebalancing to match changing economic climates or personal goals (essentially just rearranging the deck chairs). If you seek the advice of an adviser or google "how to invest," you will learn that you should be heavily weighted to stocks in your younger years, with just a bit of fixed-income to diversify the portfolio (how diversified can you really be with just two investment classes?) and then gradually reweight your allocations until your portfolio is nearly all fixed-income as you approach retirement age. If you have a higher risk tolerance, you might want to invest in riskier stocks, such as those in emerging industries or countries. If you want to boost your fixed-income returns, you can look at B-grade or junk bonds. But in the end, it is still all stocks and bonds.

You can invest directly or through mutual funds. You can use a 401(k) plan or rely on a corporate pension plan. You can even use online programs such as Acorns that take your change and invest in a balanced portfolio. But in the end, it is all stocks and bonds, no matter how you balance or how what vehicles you use to invest.

The problem with this strategy is that it doesn't account for changes in the economy or investment environment, and it requires the investor to constantly be trying to figure out the best mix of just two asset classes. When everything is going well—when GDP is growing and consumer confidence is high—stocks also typically do well. I was going to say stocks are a great investment during this type of economic climate, but I don't really think they are a great investment at any time. They are always volatile. You can lose everything overnight. If you have to sell immediately to cover an unexpected expense, you never know what the price will be. An awful lot of people who thought they'd be able to retire in 2008 and 2009, based on the equity returns they were getting in 2006 or 2007, are still working today. As Father Guido Sarducci might say, "The market giveth and the market taketh away." And people invariably buy at the wrong time—they jump in when stocks are high and pull out when they are low.

After the financial crisis, once the economy stabilized and equities began to rise off the bottom, the stock market set record after record, year after year. It was hard to find a loser in the bunch. Much of this upswing was driven by the algorithms supporting computerized passive investing. Private and institutional investors alike now use computer models to invest, and—according to computer logic—one of the strongest indications that people should buy more stocks is that the market is going up. As long as the market continues to rise, more capital is thrown into it via these passive investment engines, guaranteeing that the market continues to go up. A lot of these buy/sell decisions are programmed into computers that execute transactions automatically, with no specific human input. At some point, however, the trend turns, and the same engines that fueled the record-breaking climb will also fuel a record-breaking decline as their models tell them to sell, sell, sell. Now, not only do *people* tend to buy high and sell low, *computers* tend to do the same thing.

The bond side isn't much better. You typically won't lose your principal if you invest in treasuries or AAA-rated bonds, but you have no control over the interest rates or returns. You take what they give you. Also, you think you're making money, but in reality, you're often *losing* money if you adjust for inflation. And just as the stock market was setting record highs after the recession, bonds were stuck in historically low territory, bouncing along the bottom for years.

The frustrating and stubborn low rates were primarily a function of the federal government seeking to unfreeze the finance markets after the crash. In an effort to provide cash to the country's mortgage and lending markets, the Federal Reserve took the unusual step of increasing the money supply by buying huge amounts of treasuries and commercial mortgage-backed securities (CMBSs), a strategy that has become known as *quantitative easing* and resulted in interest rates being driven down by government purchases rather than a normal supply-and-demand dynamic. Theoretically, increasing the money supply and lowering rates should make it easier for banks to lend. That means it should be easier for businesses to borrow, which in turn means the economy should recover faster than if left to its own devices. The strategy eventually worked as planned, but it also resulted in almost a decade of negligible fixed-income returns.

And yet, despite the low interest rates we all suffered through after the recession, there is something comforting about knowing exactly how much you are going to receive from your investments each month. In addition, bonds have typically been touted as the best defense against a falling stock market. Fixed-income investments might not provide the razzle-dazzle growth returns of high-flying stocks, but they also won't leave you stranded by crashing and burning. But buying bonds when interest rates are low is rarely a good move, because low-rate bonds lose their value as rates begin to rise—which they always do, eventually. If you are happy to hold your bonds until maturity, then rate movement doesn't matter too much. But if you want to sell a bond before it matures, you will likely have to sell at a discount, because buyers know they can buy higher-rate bonds elsewhere.

Despite the drawbacks to both major investment classes, a diversified portfolio usually contains both of them—and it should. They really do complement each other, as one does better when the other is struggling. Having bonds in your portfolio helps cushion the impact of a falling stock market, while including stocks helps boost returns when fixed-income rates are threatening to go negative.

The problem I see really isn't the two classes themselves (even if I think the typical investor's emphasis on stocks is misplaced); it's the focus on them as the *only* way to invest. Experts will usually tell clients to buy stocks in good economic times and to buy bonds when the economy is struggling. That sounds simple enough, but finding the optimal risk/return sweet spot is rarely simple. To be successful with this strategy, you need to know what the future will bring to determine the best time to rebalance your portfolio and capitalize on the advantages of the rising asset class while mitigating the drawbacks of the struggling asset class.

Unless you are a professional investor, you probably don't want to have to rebalance your portfolio every time the economy takes a turn, either up or down. You don't want to always be thinking about your investments. You undoubtedly have a day job, a family, and other interests that you'd prefer to focus on. But even if you like starting each morning looking at what the Asian markets did overnight and using spreadsheets to determine exactly how each slight movement has affected your portfolio, you would need the foresight of the Oracle at Delphi to consistently predict the exact moment the market will turn. Professional investors have long known that trying to time the market is a fool's errand.

AN INVESTMENT THAT SPANS
THE GOOD AND BAD TIMES

Wouldn't it be great if there was an investment that was right for all economic climates? One that would give security of income while providing an interest rate several percentage points above treasuries and other highly-rated bonds? One that you didn't have to pull back from just because US GDP was slowing to a crawl or, conversely, flying high?

In case you haven't noticed, this whole book has been talking about just such an investment—non-conventional lending.

As I write this book early in 2018, the markets are looking suspiciously like those of 2007. A lot of people are relying on the cheap money being funneled into the economy by the Fed. These investors are buying more real estate and other real assets than they would normally, because they can afford the monthly payments. Even with President Trump's tax plan passing, the gap between median income and housing prices is growing larger each year.

So far, things have worked well for these buyers. Real estate values have now reached pre-crisis levels in nearly all major markets and have exceeded 2007 peaks in the most competitive markets— and investors are still buying. Those who stocked up on real estate when prices and financing rates were low are making a killing by selling to those who want to get in now. It's hard to look at the exuberance surrounding real estate's return and not feel a bit of deja vu. The low rates that have driven the increase in prices aren't sustainable. We already saw the Fed recently raise rates, and they will undoubtedly keep raising them in the near term until the Fed has sold off the bonds it owns and unravels the quantitative easing—unless, of course, raising rates cause the economy to tank again, because all those investors with low-rate financing find themselves unable to make their payments. Unwinding the quantitative easing mechanism is new territory for the Fed—it has never been in this position before. How selling all those fixed-income instruments on the open market will affect the economy is anyone's guess. My guess is that it is going to hurt.

In addition, it isn't just real estate loans we need to worry about. Regulations were put in place to try to prevent the type of subprime mortgage lending that led to the housing crash from spiraling out of control again, as well as discourage the types of securitization that resulted in CMBSs, CDOs (collateralized debt obligations), CMOs (collateralized mortgage obligations), and other alphabet vehicles that sliced and diced mortgages until they were no longer associated with any semblance of the underlying real estate. For the most part, these regulations have worked. Banks have been much more conservative in making home loans, and the investment banks have seen securitization vehicles like CMBS curtailed.

But humans have a way of just going down another path when one is blocked. We aren't seeing out-of-control mortgage lending, but we *are* seeing the same type of subprime lending that rocked the mortgage industry leaking into the auto industry. Look around you the next time you drive on the highway. You will note that nearly all the cars are relatively new and probably well into the $30,000-plus category. In fact, the average cost of a new car in April 2017 was more than $33,500, according to Kelley Blue Book. That means that under normal circumstances, the driver of an average new car put down $6,700 (20 percent of $33,500) and financed the remaining $26,500 at about 3.5 percent (if they had perfect credit) over forty-eight months, for a monthly payment of about $600.[22] Taxes and fees are usually added on to the down payment, making the initial cash outlay several hundred dollars—or in some high-tax states, several thousand dollars—more. Do you believe that all of those new car owners flying past you in the fast lane had thousands of dollars

---

22 "Average Auto Loan Interest Rates: 2017 Facts & Figures," ValuePenguin, https://www.valuepenguin.com/auto-loans/average-auto-loan-interest-rates.

available for a down payment, excellent credit, and the ability to pay $600 a month? I don't either.

But lucky for them, they don't have to. Lenders have been loosening their underwriting standards to qualify buyers with less-than-great income or credit scores for extra-low interest rates, and thus lower payments. Every dealer on auto row is offering nothing-down loans. Seven-year payment terms are becoming the norm, which makes the monthly payment affordable. Adjustable-rate loans and balloon loans have entered the mainstream market (sound familiar?). Lenders have even developed a class of "very credit-chal-lenged" borrowers that they call *deep subprime*. I can almost hear analysts saying five years from now, "Anyone who could fog a wind-shield could get a loan."

With the low interest rates of the past few years, these auto loans have been working out relatively well. They've even been securitized, in much the same way commercial real estate mortgages were, into auto-backed securities. As we moved into 2018, however, lenders began to see defaults, particularly on their deep subprime loans, according to Equifax.[23] New car prices were falling, meaning lenders who repossess cars are unlikely to recover the loan value. It's all just too reminiscent of the run-up to the real estate crisis to ignore.

At the risk of people who are reading this book several years from now pointing out how wrong I was back in 2018 (*Chicken Little* comes to mind), I'm going to predict that we will see another financial crisis by 2020. The subprime mortgage market set off a domino effect that pulled down the entire financial services industry. Defaults in the subprime auto loan industry could snowball into a

---

23   Adam Tempkin, "Deep Subprime Car Loans Hit Crisi-Era Milestone," *Bloomberg*, Aug. 15, 2017, https://www.bloomberg.com/news/articles/2017-08-15/-deep-subprime-car-loans-hit-crisis-era-milestone-as-woes-mount.

downturn that sends the auto industry spiraling. As the mortgage crisis showed us, our world is so globalized and every industry seems interdependent. We are now so intertwined that weakness in one often exacerbates weaknesses in other. A failure in the auto industry might not have the long-term effect that frozen financial markets had, but you will feel it.

It's in this type of uncertain economic environment that real estate and non-conventional lending shine (actually, non-conventional lending shines in any economy, but you get my point). Looking at what is happening in all the financial markets, as well as consumer spending and debt levels, I think we need to prepare for a downturn. It is also possible that the Fed's rate increases could get out of hand, however, and we'll be in the middle of an inflationary period in a couple of years. But honestly, the climate doesn't matter. Non-conventional lending is appropriate and profitable in any economic environment, whether we're dealing with inflation, deflation, or stagnation.

THE BEST OF SEVERAL WORLDS

Non-conventional loans stand up in any climate, because they offer the diversity and advantages of real estate with the safety of being in a debt position (rather than owning it). Diversifying into hard assets—e.g., real estate—is a well-known strategy used by institutional investors to reduce risk while increasing returns in a multi-asset-class portfolio.

Real estate is still technically considered an alternative investment, but you'd be hard-pressed to find any institutional portfolio without at least a few percentage points of real estate. Most aim for about 10 percent of the portfolio, with some foundations and endowments having allocations up to 25 percent. There are many reasons underpinning real estate's move to a mainstream asset class. And that's really real estate's advantage—it doesn't have one benefit; it has many.

- **Income**—Real estate is first and foremost an income-producing asset. In good times and bad, investors can count on rent payments—as long they did their due diligence and rented to a creditworthy tenant. For many investors, the income is the only reason to invest in real estate. They don't care if the property depreciates in value as long as the income continues to flow.

- **Appreciation**—Historically, rental properties have appreciated with inflation. But these properties also appreciated in the far-from-inflationary years that followed the Great Recession, because the universe of renters increased as lost employment and stagnant wages reduced household income and priced many out of the housing market. This value appreciation is an added benefit when paired with the income characteristic.

- **Inflation hedge**—Rental properties are considered an inflation hedge, because rents can be increased as expenses rise, while mortgage payments remain the same. When inflation goes up, it can also mean more renters, as mortgages become more expensive for average consumers. More renters increase demand, so rents can escalate. Because leases are typically renewed annually, you can count on increased rent each year. For those who favor month-to-month contracts, costs can be recovered even sooner. Owners of rental real estate rarely get left behind as inflation takes off.

Private investors have been a little slow to jump into real assets, but they have been making up for lost time since the real estate crash. About 23 percent of residential homes built for one to four families are now owned by investors, according to the Iceberg Report, a 2017 study published by REAL Trends and NEXZUS Publishing Group. The vast majority of those homes are owned by individual investors or small investment groups. The study found that institutional owners actually own fewer than 400,000 single-family residential homes, while nearly 8 million non-institutional investors own the rest.

There are several ways to become one of these 8 million non-institutional investors. Most probably use equity to pay the down payment on the residence and then take out a mortgage to finance the rest. You could do the same thing, or you could be the person supplying the financing. It should be obvious that this is the tact I think you should use. I'd prefer to be the banker and get paid interest on my loan than to be paying the banker for a loan.

As mentioned in an earlier chapter, one of the best ways to access real estate is through real estate financing. By providing the financing (i.e. the mortgage), you not only get the advantages of real estate's portfolio diversifying characteristics, but also significantly reduce the risk by hanging out in a more secure part of the capital stack. Investing in loans *secured* by real estate, rather than supplying the equity, puts you in a position to be paid back before the equity is returned, as well as naming your price for providing the financing to the equity provider. That's an investment that is hard to beat.

If someone asked me to describe the strategy in tweet-worthy language, I'd simply say, "Non-conventional lending combines the advantages of real estate with the advantages of fixed-income vehicles and overlays the benefits that come from being in complete control of the investment." (Luckily, they've expanded the Twitter character count.) You choose the asset. You negotiate repayment terms and interest rates. You determine what to do if the property goes into default.

Non-conventional lending has other characteristics that make it perfect for all economic environments. Because the loan term is typically short, it is rare that anything in the macro- or microeconomic world surrounding the real estate collateral would change between the start of the loan and the payoff. This means you can feel confident that the terms you negotiate will provide the return you expect.

One of the characteristics of non-conventional lending that sets it apart from other investment sectors is the control the investor maintains. When you are investing in stocks, you can spend weeks researching individual companies or funds. You can fill out pages and pages of spreadsheets. But after you invest your capital, you are at the mercy of a market that moves on rumors and emotion more than logic. People jump in when it is high, only to jump out on the basis of news stories and events that have nothing to do with the companies they've invested in. It's awfully hard to predict an annual return for your portfolio when you can't control the investment.

An often-overlooked advantage to non-conventional lending is the personal relationship that lenders and borrowers often develop. Entrepreneurs, such as professional real estate rehabbers, typically use private loans for multiple properties. These relationships allow both the lender and borrower to navigate any hiccups with the best interest of both sides in mind. The relationship is less confrontational and more collegial than you'll find with most institutional lenders.

All these benefits don't mean investors can throw caution to the wind, however. While I believe non-conventional loans can be less risky than stocks and provide better returns than other fixed-income products, and while you can count on the returns in good times and bad, you still need to handle these investments with care. Knowing your market is crucial. Doing your due diligence on both the property and the borrower is crucial. Having a broker and legal professionals in your corner who are experts in non-conventional lending is crucial. In other words, investors need to be cautious and know what they are doing.

Now is a time to be extra cautious. I'm seeing some things in the market that are beginning to concern me. Some lenders are going up to 80 percent LTV of the ARV. That's an issue; the LTV should be much lower, to protect your investment, and it should be based on the purchase price. Some are lending at 6 percent interest rate. That's an issue; it should be higher than standard mortgage rates to pay you for the risk you are taking. Rehab loans are seeing competition and compression. That's an issue; while market competition keeps people honest, too much of it drives down interest rates or loosens underwriting standards, meaning you are taking on more risk than you should.

These issues aren't insurmountable, however. Many of these issues are the result of competition for the best assets, because it is hard to find product in some of the best markets. If the non-conventional loan industry were larger and more diverse, many of the excesses would be smoothed. With a larger pool of assets to finance, LTVs would likely revert to a relatively conservative 75 percent of the purchase price, or even a truly conservative 65 percent. Interest rates would increase to a more reasonable level. If there was a way for those who had capital to find those who needed capital—whether in their local markets or elsewhere—the non-conventional lending industry would grow exponentially.

I probably don't need to tell you that I have some ideas that reflect how we can make it easier for lenders and borrowers to connect. All it takes is a virtual exchange platform. And I know where you can find one.

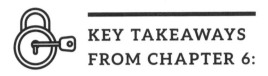

KEY TAKEAWAYS FROM CHAPTER 6:

1. Stocks and bonds have their place in your portfolio, but the new norm is to have non-conventional loans there as well.

2. Advisers only tell you about stocks and bonds, because that's all they know. Interested in more? Find RIAs who understand non-conventional lending on our exchange site: http://www.nonconexchange.com.

TAKE ACTION *NOW*

1. Go to Non-Conventional Lending Guide and Non-Conventional Lending Exchange to find RIAs who understand this space. Talk to them about how to invest in these loans.

2. Educate yourself: Talk with the RIAs on the list, talk with brokers who lend in this space, and talk to regular RIAs who invest in stocks and bonds. What's right for you?

Check out these websites for more information:

Non-Conventional Lending Guide Chapter 6: http://www.nonconlendingguide.com/chapter6

Originate Report (to network with non-conventional lenders): http://www.originate.report

Educate yourself at a GeraciCon conference:
http://www.geracicon.com

Get on the exchange: http://www.nonconexchange.com

KEY QUESTION:

How skilled do you feel about non-conventional lending, on a scale of one to ten?

CHAPTER 7

IN CASE OF EMERGENCY, BREAK GLASS: IF STUFF HAPPENS, CASE STUDIES, STORIES, AND MORE

Right around this time, I bet you're thinking, "It's too good to be true," because everything I've said is that you get a high-yield return, do nothing, and get money. Of course, stuff happens, and there can definitely be delays, issues, and more. But in all of my years investing, I've never lost money investing in non-conventional loans. Not because I'm a savant or smarter than other people, mind you, but I have learned by observation—watching where my clients made mistakes and avoiding those pitfalls at all costs. That's not to say I haven't had to invest additional monies to protect my interest in these loans.

As I've said before, I invest heavily in this space. I like to do second-lien mortgages. These aren't for everyone, but they are for people who like additional risk for additional rewards. I thought I'd share a few case studies about when loans went wrong, what I did about it, and how I ended up making more money when things went wrong than when they went right.

THE CASE OF THE BORROWER WHO DIDN'T WANT TO PAY AND BOUNCED CHECKS

I made a loan to a borrower—we'll call him Steve—in North Hollywood, California. The property in question was in good condition, and it was unique in the sense that the houses around it were 1,200 square feet, but this one was 3,700 square feet, with a main home and a casita (Spanish for "little house"). The property appraised for $1.2 million, and Steve was looking for a $175,000 second lien for business purposes. There was a first lien on the property for $750,000, made by a bank at a 4 percent interest rate per annum. After making sure Steve submitted proof that the first lien was current, I decided it was a good transaction. For those of you who do the math, you'll find that the combined LTV of the first and second liens was 72.6 percent, which was within my tolerance for the loan. We agreed to a 14 percent interest rate, and we were off to the races.

Until, that is, Steve's first check bounced. I called him when I learned of it, and he apologized and promised to send me a replacement. He didn't. After a further call, I told him I would have to foreclose on his property if he didn't pay. He overnighted me two checks, one for the (now) missed month and one for his payment due. Again, both checks bounced. I called Steve again; he told me they shouldn't have bounced. I asked for him to send me a money order, wire, or cashier's check; any of those would have guaranteed the funds were good. No surprise to you, I didn't receive anything. He left me with no choice but to protect my investment, and I started foreclosure. I also charged him a default interest rate 6 percentage points higher than the 14 percent (or 20 percent total), which is legal in California.

At the time of foreclosure, in California, the foreclosure laws require us to file a notice of default and give the borrower ninety days before setting a Notice of Sale. The entire foreclosure process could be completed as soon as 111 days, by law. I hired a good law firm to file the foreclosure. Right around the time the property was going to sale, the borrower filed bankruptcy. While it appears scary, this is a fairly common tactic taught to borrowers' attorneys. Since my lien had equity, there was no chance of bankruptcy affecting my lien. It did, however, delay the sale, as bankruptcy has an automatic stay on all legal matters against the borrower. Our attorneys got a motion for relief granted; the borrower dismissed his bankruptcy and filed another one, with another automatic stay. Again, our attorneys got bankruptcy relief, and we again got relief from the automatic stay. Then, the borrower dismissed for the third time, refiled bankruptcy, and separately sued me in state court for a variety of matters.

I know what you're thinking: "WHAT?! There's no way I'm doing this! Look at all the attorneys' fees you spent!" You would be right—I did spend money on attorneys' fees, especially since I don't practice much as an attorney

> nowadays. However, almost every note has an attorneys'
> fees clause baked into it, which says that attorneys' fees
> can be added to the note if for collection purposes. To me
> (and every state court I've reviewed agrees), when the
> borrower is actively preventing recovery, these legal fees
> are collection-related expenses, and thus, the borrower
> effectively pays for these attorneys' fees.

To make a long story short, we successfully defended the baseless lawsuit the borrower made, ended up foreclosing, and collected *every dollar of interest, including the default interest, attorneys' fees, costs, and principal owed to me.*

THE CASE OF THE BAD LOAN AND THE INVESTOR WHO REALLY WANTED THE PROPERTY

I had another loan in Northern California where the borrower similarly defaulted on the first payment and went incommunicado. We began the foreclosure process, but that didn't even prompt the borrower to call me. I thought it was strange, because when you start the foreclosure process most borrowers start to wake up. This one didn't.

I got to the Notice of Sale and still didn't hear from the borrower. At this point my mind is racing—was this fraudulent? Did I miss something? I basically re-underwrote the loan and concluded that everything checked out and was in line with what I understood. The loan was 70 percent CLTV, there was plenty of equity in it, and even with adding the missed payments, I would fully recoup my investment in foreclosure. It just didn't make sense.

In any event, someone who was watching the foreclosure reached out to me and asked if I would be interested in selling my loan to her. I'm not in the business of owning single-family residences, so I told her I would consider it, but I wouldn't consider anything less than par. *Par* means what I was owed at the time of when the buyer wanted to buy the loan. The buyer was very interested in it, and it was her hope that she would get the property in foreclosure. The LTV looked good, so I doubted she would, but I was more than happy to sell her my loan because I could recover my investment now versus waiting 2 months to complete the foreclosure. We closed on the transaction in seven days, and I moved on to the next loan.

THE CASE OF NON-CONVENTIONAL LENDING HELPING PEOPLE

I refinanced an elderly lady who owned a duplex as an investment (i.e., she did not live in it). She was in danger of being foreclosed on and had fallen behind on payments for the duplex. It was an absolutely gorgeous property in Long Beach, California near the ocean. My LTV was 52 percent, and we were able to negotiate a 13 percent interest rate. More tangible than the interest rate, loan amount and property was that the woman was genuinely thankful to receive the loan. Every payment was on time and she wrote me a handwritten note during every month that contained a holiday.

She was late a few times, but because of how sweet she was, I waived the late fee. She told me she used the extra money in the refinance to fix up the property. When she sold it, she told me that because of my loan she was able to sell the property for $200,000 more than if she did not get my loan. She was incredibly friendly, thoughtful and did everything she agreed to.

In my experience, you have to take the credibility of the borrower into account.

KEY TAKEAWAYS FROM CHAPTER 7:

1. Stuff happens. Be prepared for it. Set some money aside if you own non-conventional loans to advance attorneys' fees and foreclosure fees—you'll collect them later if your note has an attorneys' fees clause. (And it should have one!)

2. Don't look to own the property. I make these loans as investments, not to own the properties, but there's a reason these loans are secured by a property. If the borrower doesn't fulfill their promises, it's the collateral I have to protect the loan I made.

3. Hire good advisers: an attorney, broker, and investment adviser who specialize in non-conventional loans. They're not just your vendors; they're your partners and are worth their weight in gold.

4. Don't believe people's words—believe their actions. If they send a check and it clears, remove the foreclosure and collect the win!

TAKE ACTION *NOW*

1. Think about your ability to foreclose on someone. If it makes you squeamish, think about investing passively and letting someone else do the work. If it doesn't, think about becoming

an active investor and buying these notes directly from an exchange.

2. Do the work. Review the loan documents and files. Do they all make sense? If so, buy the loan, and set aside some cash in case you need to fight a borrower who just doesn't want to work with you.

Check out these websites for more information:

Non-Conventional Lending Guide Chapter 7:
http://www.nonconlendingguide.com/chapter7

Originate Report (to network with non-conventional lenders):
http://www.originate.report

Educate yourself at a GeraciCon conference:
http://www.geracicon.com

Get on the exchange: http://www.nonconexchange.com

KEY QUESTION:

On a scale of one to ten, how much more comfortable do you feel knowing you can recoup any costs you advance (including attorneys' fees) that a borrower costs you to get your money back?

CHAPTER 8

THE FUTURE OF NON-CONVENTIONAL LENDING

If you've read this far, you must have started to wonder why an investment with as many benefits as non-conventional lending isn't more popular. Why aren't more high-net-worth individuals, family offices, and other private investors involved? It's a question I'm asked almost daily as I handle my own investments or the legal processes for others.

The answer is simple. Presently, there is no easy way for lenders and borrowers to find each other.

As I mentioned earlier, these deals typically are funneled through brokers or attorneys who have become experts through experience. Each deal is a one-off transaction, so neither the investor nor the borrower really knows if the loan terms and interest rate are typical for the market. While some see this as a benefit, because it means each participant is able to negotiate any terms they want, most prefer to know what standard terms typically entail and to negotiate from there.

One way to solve the problem of investors and borrowers passing in the night is to develop an exchange or trading platform where each participant could find an appropriate counterpart. The stock market is the perfect example of what happens when such a platform is introduced.

Today, stocks and bonds are the foundation of a diversified portfolio. I'd be willing to bet that anyone who has invested in anything—that is, has done more than put cash in a savings account—has owned at least some stock, whether directly or through mutual funds, 401(k) plans, or pension funds. But it wasn't always that way. At one time, investors concentrated on bonds, with only the most adventurous dabbling in stocks. People looking for investments bought savings bonds and tucked them inside their Bibles or under their mattresses for safekeeping.

The stock market, on the other hand, was put in the same category as panning for gold. Only wildcatters participated. Some might make a ton of money, but it certainly wasn't the place for a family man to put his hard-earned money. The stock market crash of 1929, which was caused by a market fueled by speculation and corporate corruption, didn't do anything to dispel this perception of the stock market, nor did it help the case for broader adoption by the private, everyday investor.

It wasn't until the stock exchanges grew, standardized, and became more transparent that securities became the foundation of every investor's portfolio.

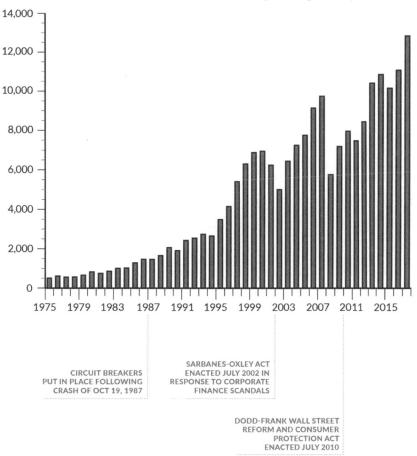

NYSE COMPOSITE INDEX
Investor Confidence is Increased by Transparency

CIRCUIT BREAKERS PUT IN PLACE FOLLOWING CRASH OF OCT 19, 1987

SARBANES-OXLEY ACT ENACTED JULY 2002 IN RESPONSE TO CORPORATE FINANCE SCANDALS

DODD-FRANK WALL STREET REFORM AND CONSUMER PROTECTION ACT ENACTED JULY 2010

SOURCE: NYSE | NOTE: Composite data as of last day of trading for each year.

WHAT EXCHANGES/PLATFORMS HAVE DONE FOR EQUITIES

The history of the stock exchanges is one of a series of rules and regulations being adopted to improve efficiency and build shareholder confidence. Most of the improvements were forced upon the exchanges and the corporations that trade on them after major dislocations—such as the implementation of the Securities Acts of 1933 and 1934 following the Great Depression; the implementation of circuit breakers following Black Monday in 1987; the passing of the Sarbanes-Oxley Act following the Enron and MCI scandals in the early 2000s—but without fail, as the regulations were implemented, the exchanges saw jumps in the composite index, as well as in trading volumes.

Transparency and trust in the markets undoubtedly increased the number of investors willing to participate in the exchanges. In addition to the improvement in corporate governance promoted by regulations, technological advances have improved efficiency, both in the trading markets themselves and in the ability of investors to do their due diligence.

The use of electronic trading, which originally was limited to how the exchanges processed transactions from licensed brokers, greatly improved efficiency and broker productivity. As computerized trading spread through the industry, the exchanges were able to increase volumes without a corresponding increase in the number of brokers. In 1970, for example, the average number of trades per day per broker was 88. By 2006, the average number had soared to 2,624. Today, it is not unusual to see brokers process more than three thousand trades per day.[24] Comparisons are a bit hard to make—in the early days, all trades were made by floor dealers, while today much of the trading is done online by investors themselves—but the trend is obvious: Move a trading process onto a digital platform, and the volume of trades skyrockets.

---

24 "Occupational Outlook Handbook—Securities, Commodities, and Financial Services Sales Agents" US Bureau of Labor Statistics, https://www.bls.gov/ooh/sales/securities-commodities-and-financial-services-sales-agents.htm#tab-1; "Markets Data Center," *The Wall Street Journal*, http://online.wsj.com/mdcapp/public/page/marketsdata.html

Today, individual investors can go online and buy, sell, and otherwise transact in real time. As investors have found themselves closer to the action—in other words, they aren't calling up a broker, who then calls a floor trader, who then makes a bid—they have become more comfortable with making their own decisions, and the transaction volume has grown significantly.

Of course, some of this increase in speed is the result of data simply being transmitted faster along digital highways than brokers could transmit on the telephone or face-to-face. But an awful lot of the efficiency and trust in the system are by-products of technology: standardization and transparency.

To work efficiently, data must be inputted into systems in a standardized format. With standardized input comes standardized output. Brokers, buyers, and sellers can now all receive reports in the same format. Comparisons among stocks and companies are much easier than when investors had to search through reports in varying formats and manipulate data themselves to produce usable information. As investing in the stock market became easier and more transparent—and thus more reliable—the universe of investors expanded. You no longer had to be a financial whiz with the math skills of an MIT professor to compare various offerings and decide which ones fit your portfolio. You simply had to access a standardized prospectus and compare it to another standardized prospectus.

Standardizing huge amounts of data also led to vastly improved transparency. Irregularities could no longer hide among the apples and oranges of incomparable numbers. Investors might go on to make their own, individualized comparisons, but at least everyone was starting at the same place. When common investors came to believe that they weren't being railroaded by speculators and robber barons, they became much more likely to be comfortable participating in the market.

The improvement in trading transparency and the resulting reduction in risk also corresponded to a significant increase in US institutional ownership of equities. In exchange for their large capital commitments, the first wave of institutional investors demanded improved corporate governance and even greater transparency, which in return allowed additional financial institutions to invest in stocks. As institutional ownership increased, the equities markets were forced to standardize reports, open board of directors meetings, and meet other demands for corporate governance improvements. Despite the often-slow implementation of standards, they have proved to be extremely beneficial to the industry.

But maybe the best thing the exchanges did to promote the industry was to make it easy for those with shares to sell to connect with those looking to buy. In the beginning, buyers and sellers had to seek out each other through brokers, or even via the "upstairs market," where off-exchange transactions occurred. As the number of companies on the exchanges grew, and as electronic processing of transactions took over the industry, buyers and sellers could efficiently find each other, decreasing transaction costs and increasing volume.

The types of improvements that exchanges brought to the equities markets—transparency, standardization of data reporting, trustworthy information, and efficient transactions—are the same improvement that investors in non-conventional lending are looking for. All it will take is someone to step forward and develop a workable platform. It seems obvious that we could look to the template already developed by the equities exchanges, but things are never that simple. The devil, as always, will be in the details.

TECHNOLOGY'S ROLE IN PROMOTING STANDARDS

The importance of technology isn't just in its ability to speed up the transaction process—it's also in its ability to standardize the acquisitions, due diligence, and disposition arenas and thus promote the transparency, efficiency, and credibility needed to attract investors. Industries with standardized systems are viewed more favorably by the public, government regulators, and industry participants, thus actually allowing the industry more freedom in how it conducts its business, as well as increasing potential profits.

The use of technology and a trading platform could be the single most effective method of promoting the standards necessary for the non-conventional lending industry to grow. Today, nearly all investors, sellers, and brokers use digitized information to speed transactions in the equities and bonds markets, but this collection of data does little more than transfer information faster. To really affect how the industry does business, information must be used and stored in a centralized location, just as stocks are traded on a centralized stock exchange.

Real estate has always been a local, individualized investment. As such, it has shied away from electronic exchanges in favor of face-to-face transactions. But for the non-conventional lender and borrower, the advantages of face-to-face transactions pale in comparison to the disadvantages in trying to achieve such meetings.

The advantages of a central clearinghouse swept the stock market from speculative investment territory to the foundation of retirement portfolios. It can do even more for non-conventional lending.

BENEFITS OF A CENTRAL EXCHANGE
FOR NON-CONVENTIONAL LENDING

First and foremost, a central clearinghouse and exchange would overcome the major stumbling block in growing the universe of non-conventional lending participants: connecting lenders with borrowers. But the advantage doesn't come just from connecting one borrower with one lender. It also comes from allowing multiple lenders to get in front of multiple borrowers, and multiple borrowers to negotiate with multiple lenders. It's this ability to access the full universe of lenders or borrowers, rather than just one or two, that will turn non-conventional lending into a mainstream alternative the same way that equity real estate is now in nearly every institutional portfolio and that REITs have given the everyday investor access to the benefits of real estate.

When lenders and borrowers have access to multiple participants across the table—or along the digital highway—good things happen. Both the lender and borrower are able to compare and contrast terms, and the clearinghouse is able to record the terms of each deal, making standard terms more obvious. When everyone knows what is typical, transparency improves and investors feel more comfortable lending their capital. Borrowers, too, are more comfortable, because they know what to expect. Newcomers to any investment class often feel that they are being taken advantage of by the more experienced practitioners. The better the transparency, the more comfortable everyone feels, and the bigger the universe will be.

Along with this transparency comes efficiency. We've all heard the phrase, "time is money." That is particularly true when it comes to investments. The longer capital remains in a savings account or under your mattress (where it essentially earns the same interest as a savings account), the lower your annual returns will be. You want to find an appropriate borrower, come to terms quickly, and get that capital out earning its keep.

A central clearinghouse improves efficiency by allowing the collection of data in one spot. As multiple transactions are completed, the terms that underlie each one can be aggregated so that, over time, a clearer picture of the industry begins to appear. A range of typical interest rates will form. Standard payback terms will evolve. Normal LTV ratios will fall in line. Investors will be able to look at the average transaction and decide if they want to offer loans at a lower rate, higher LTV values, or more flexible repayment terms than normal—or if they want to adhere to the standard. Borrowers will have a better idea of what is normal and therefore will be more comfortable when it comes to negotiating terms. All this makes for a more transparent, efficient, and growing industry in which investors and borrowers alike feel confident that they can trust each other.

As time goes on, this collection of data could also be used to pinpoint any problem areas that need attention, as well as provide possible solutions. It's impossible to solve a problem if it can't be defined. Without standardized, unbiased data, it is very difficult to define financial market problems.

Conversely, of course, it could also be used to pinpoint areas that are working well. This type of data would help players ascertain which types of borrowers are most likely to fulfill their obligations. It helps lenders determine what interest rates they should be charging to cover each level of risk. It helps lenders perform adequate due diligence. On the other hand, it helps borrowers know when lenders are offering typical terms and when they are offering expensive money. All in all, real-time, unbiased data is good for both lenders and borrowers and for the industry as a whole.

An exchange will not only expand the universe of investors and borrowers, making it more likely that each will find a better fit for their needs, but will also expand the geographic reach of each participant. Real estate has always been a local investment. In fact, you won't find a real estate person who doesn't espouse that axiom. It's based on the very real notion that real estate performance is tied much more to local market dynamics than to macro factors. But non-conventional lending is different. While the underlying real estate is crucial, you aren't as concerned about future performance as an equity investor would be. You simply want your loan paid back. You've set up specific terms to make sure that happens. Whether the property is eventually leased or meets appreciation expectations isn't your concern. As such, what is happening in the local market isn't as relevant as what is happening to this particular property and the ability of the borrower to meet repayment terms.

A virtual exchange is perfect for breaking down the geographic boundaries that aren't a factor for non-conventional lending. Using an Internet-based platform, an investor in California who might want to supply financing for a property in Florida could now do so. Because borrowers and investors from all over the country would be on the exchange, it should be easy to find potential borrowers in other states. The lender, of course, would need to be aware of local laws and regulations. A good exchange would contain a directory of brokers and attorneys, broken out by city or state, who are experienced in non-conventional lending. A local attorney is important when you are dealing with local property. It is crucial when you are dealing with property in a different state.

The important thing to note is that an exchange would make all of this relatively easy. You could connect with a borrower, find an experienced local broker, do a quick overview of the property from afar, and hire an experienced local attorney to guide you through local regulations and customs—all from your computer screen. It's possible to do all that now, but it's certainly not easy.

"And why would I want to invest outside my local area?" you might ask. Remember earlier when I mentioned that interest rates and returns are compressing because of competition in some of the most active areas of the country? California is the poster child for this. If you had access to other areas of the country where there also are well-located properties, but with less competition on the lending side, you would be able to charge a higher interest rate and thus realize better returns. Why wouldn't you want to do that?

Of course, investing across state lines brings its own concerns. Each state has its own rules and regulations. Some require private lenders to be licensed. Others don't. Some limit how much interest you can charge. Others don't. The time to foreclose can vary drastically. The average time to foreclose on a property in New York, for example, is 445 days. Other states, such as Texas, average less than one hundred days. But finding ways to accommodate these differences can be well worth it. According to a sampling of mortgage funds in 2015, those restricted to just one state (California) averaged 7 percent returns, while multi-state funds were returning 13 percent.

A good, local attorney and broker will help you navigate any local lending requirements. And an active non-conventional lending platform would have well-populated directories to put you touch with those local professionals.

PLATFORM WITH AN EDUCATIONAL FRAMEWORK

What good is a platform, though, if it doesn't train you? A proper platform should have resources and tools on it so you can learn the industry no matter how new you are, and you shouldn't have to go to the latest guru to get trained and part with $25,000 a year to figure it out.

Part of an exchange is the ability to exchange information as well.

NOW THE HARD PART

The easy part in this exercise is to spot the problems. I've been making non-conventional loans for a long time and have spent a lot of time trying to pinpoint the roadblocks to expanding the participant universe. It's a bit of a vicious cycle. Most of the issues come from the fact that investors and borrowers don't have an easy way to find each other, but the reason they can't find each other is the lack of transparency and efficiency caused by this lack of access. Because of the opaque nature of the industry, the participants can't connect, and that opaqueness continues. We need to break through the impasse. To do that, we need to think differently.

When I started my law firm years ago, it was structured the same way all law firms are. There were principals and staff. Everyone was pretty much an independent contributor. It soon became obvious to me that this wasn't the most efficient way to run a business. I looked around and realized that there was no reason a law firm— which is just a business with law as its product—couldn't be run the same way other corporations are. So, I restructured the firm to have a president, chief financial officer, chief operations officer, and other roles that promote the growth of the business, not just the income of an individual principal. I added divisions that grew organically from the type of law we practiced, including a conference group to provide educational events for lawyers and real estate professionals interested in non-conventional lending, and a consulting division that is finding capital for our private lending clients. We also have a publication focused on our specialties.

Thinking differently about how to structure my firm has resulted in a much better firm, where lawyers are free to practice law rather than run the business, and business people are free to focus on the business full time, rather than as a side line to their law careers. The simple thought that someone has to be the first to stir things up—and that person could be me—changed the trajectory of my entire law firm. And once we reach our goal of being the largest law firm nationally (if you are going to have a goal, make sure it is worthwhile), I'm confident that this restructuring of our law firm will drive the restructuring of law firms throughout the industry.

Looking at things from a different viewpoint is the basis for much of the growth in the world today. With the help of digital platforms and the Internet, Amazon has changed the way we shop. Google made encyclopedias obsolete. Uber has changed the way we hail a cab. Turo is trying to shake up the car rental industry the same way Airbnb did the hotel industry. Paypal, Venmo, Acorns, and other financial platforms have made inroads into how we bank, transfer money, and invest. The list goes on—and is getting longer by the day.

All of these disrupters had one thing in common—they looked at how we were currently performing some sort of activity and asked, "How can technology make that activity better, more efficient, and more focused on what people really want to do?" They looked at what people disliked about the current system and asked, "How can we make that better?" And then they just got at it.

Uber found that people hated waiting for a cab. So, they developed a system where there is always a car within minutes. Airbnb found that people wanted cheaper hotel rooms with more amenities, and they wanted more control on location. So, the founders developed a network of normal people willing to rent out rooms, apartments, and homes. Venmo makes splitting a check easier than ordering the meal. Acorns allows people to start investing with just a few dollars a month.

The combination of technology and looking at the non-conventional lending industry differently could change the industry the same way all of these other platforms have changed theirs.

I've spent a lot of time thinking about what the right platform would look like and how it would work. The worst thing for non-conventional lending would be to launch a platform that caused more problems than it solved. This would chase possible investors further into the shadows, rather than bringing them into the light.

So, what would it look like? We need to take the best of all the ideas out there and transform them into a digital platform that not only provides easy access for industry players but also encourages best practices in lending and transactions, makes the industry more transparent and efficient by providing data not previously aggregated, and gives participants a chance to learn from each other.

It will have a way to connect people who have money to lend with people who need money. It will have ways to qualify both lenders and borrowers. The exchange won't proclaim some borrowers qualified and others not, but it will provide a standardized format for people to enter relevant data that can be used by their counterpart to decide whether to proceed.

It will also have directories of service providers who specialize in the non-conventional lending industry—brokers, attorneys, appraisers, and others. It might be a good idea to have some sort of rating system, similar to Yelp or Uber, that would help lenders and borrowers find the professionals they need and encourage these professionals to use customer-friendly best practices.

There will be standardized data collection forms to help compare what is asked for and offered by a variety of players. On the borrower's side, the form might include credit scores, credit history, employment history, and financial status. More importantly, it would provide enough information about the collateral property for the investor to begin his or her due diligence.

On the investor side, standardized formats would provide borrowers with lenders' interest rates, LTV range, repayment terms, lending history, and any other limits a lender might have. Some lenders, for example, might focus on a specific type of property or location.

Both investors and borrowers will be able to enter their requirements and access a list of those who match those characteristics.

There would be no maximum or minimum loan amounts, no maximum or minimum credit scores or LTVs. Those details would be negotiated between lender and borrower based on what they will now know is typical for the industry, and what they are comfortable asking for and accepting.

The platform wouldn't dictate terms or who qualified and who didn't. But by providing a way for borrowers and lenders to compare rates, terms, and other data, each could find the right fit.

Perhaps just as important as providing a place to meet, the platform would provide a place for those wanting to know more about non-conventional lending. It is currently difficult to learn about the industry. A virtual platform that educates both borrowers and lenders on best practices is crucial to expanding the universe of lenders. Participants can learn from each other, as well as from lawyers and financial advisers, who would be part of the exchange membership. It would have a virtual networking component similar to LinkedIn, where members could network with others in the industry, post best practices, offer tips, and help others connect with experienced brokers, attorneys, and others with niche expertise.

At this point, I can picture you nodding your heads and agreeing that, so far, the examples as presented sound right. You can see exactly how a non-conventional lending exchange would help everyone. But you also might be thinking, "So far, all I see is hat. Where are your cattle?"

Just as I changed the trajectory of my law firm by changing how it was structured, I am changing the trajectory of the non-conventional lending industry by changing how it is structured. I created a platform to make these deals happen and for you to learn more. Check it out at http://www.NonConExchange.com, become an investor, learn the ins and outs of non-conventional lending, and if you're inclined, invest in some loans!

And we are well on our way to transforming the industry from a tiny niche in the overall real estate market to a full-blown financing arm available to anyone with the capital or collateral.

KEY TAKEAWAYS FROM CHAPTER 8:

1. A platform is absolutely essential to modernize the non-conventional lending space. We've created such a platform at http://www.nonconxchange.com.

2. You need more than a platform—you need a place to educate, stimulate, and help people become part of the non-conventional community. Find your tribe there!

TAKE ACTION *NOW*

1. Register for an account on the exchange, and explore.

2. Talk with the people on the exchange. What are their best practices? How can they help you make and purchase better loans on the exchange?

Check out these websites for more information:

Non-Conventional Lending Guide Chapter 8:
http://www.nonconlendingguide.com/chapter8

Originate Report (to network with non-conventional lenders):
http://www.originate.report

Educate yourself at a GeraciCon conference:
http://www.geracicon.com

Get on the exchange: http://www.nonconexchange.com

KEY QUESTION:

On a scale of one to ten, how comfortable investing in fixed-income products like non-conventional loans?

CHAPTER 9

EVERYONE WELCOME—NO EXPERIENCE NECESSARY

When I look back at my best and worst non-conventional lending transactions, a pattern begins to emerge. When things didn't work out as planned (and I don't mean I lost my investment, just that it maybe took longer than expected to close, or I had to take over and sell the house—which certainly has its own benefits), it was primarily because I went ahead with a transaction that I knew wasn't a great fit, but there were no other alternatives at the moment. As I've mentioned several times (are you thinking, "too many"?), this sector is still very opaque and very small compared to other investment classes. The universe of both lenders and borrowers is relatively limited. If the size of this universe was increased, the odds of successful outcomes would also be increased, because everyone would have a better chance of connecting with the right counterpart. It's a lot like Internet dating.

You might see someone who looks perfect on paper (or the screen), but somehow you don't click. If this was the only person available in the dating pool, you might continue to see each other and hope things worked out. But if there were lots of choices, you'd both wish each other well and move on to a better match.

Except for the lack of access, there is no reason that non-conventional lending shouldn't be more popular.

Approximately ten thousand Americans turned sixty-five today, and another ten thousand will turn sixty-five every day from now until 2039, according to Pew Research.[25] In the recent past sixty-five has been the age of retirement. It's still the age at which most people assume they will be able to retire—if not sooner. Reality, however, is hitting the baby boomer generation hard. Because Americans are living longer than ever, retirement is becoming increasingly expensive, causing many to keep *working* while they can. According to an AARP survey,[26] more than half of workers over the age of thirty-five say they plan to work in retirement; 35 percent of those ages sixty-five to seventy-four cite the extra income as the biggest reason why. The problem with expecting to cover retirement expenses by continuing to work past retirement age is that stuff happens. Maybe your health fails. Maybe your job is outsourced or otherwise becomes unavailable. Or maybe you just don't have the energy to keep getting up and out to work each morning. Whatever the scenario, planning on continuing to work is not a foolproof plan to pay for life after sixty-five.

---

25   D'Vera Cohn, and Paul Taylor, "Baby Boomers Approach 65 – Glumly," Pew Research Center, December 29, 2010, http://www.pewresearch.org/fact-tank/2010/12/29/baby-boomers-retire/.

26   "AARP Life Reimagined Survey Finds More People Expect to Work Longer" AARP, July 2016, https://www.aarp.org/retirement/planning-for-retirement/info-2016/survey-more-people-expect-to-work-longer-lr.html.

The purpose of saving and investing is to provide security for your family and to fund a comfortable retirement lifestyle. This is a much better strategy than believing that you will be able to continue to work indefinitely. The downside, of course, is that many of the investment options available today simply aren't going to get you where you need to be.

If you are one of the 80 percent who are not reaching your retirement goal—or simply someone who wants to reach it a little faster—non-conventional lending could be a solution.

Look at where your portfolio stands now. Be honest. You are not going to get a 25 percent annual return. It is unlikely that, over time, you will even get a 10 percent return with the standard portfolio mix. According to Vanguard, the average annual return for a balanced 50/50 portfolio going back ninety years is 8.3 percent.[27] When forecasting returns, it is better to be conservative and be pleasantly surprised than to find yourself short on cash because you were too optimistic in your expectations.

So, using a conservative return expectation of about 7 percent annually, are you going to reach your goals continuing to do what you are doing now? And that 7 percent is only if you still have many more years until retirement; that 7 percent is going to be very hard to reach in the next few years—I'd wager in the next decade—relying on stocks and bonds. Would adding a new investment vehicle, such as non-conventional lending, help? I bet it would.

Millions of investors could benefit from this investment sector if they knew about it—and if it becomes more transparent and more welcoming to newcomers. To that end, we need to open up the non-conventional lending industry so more people can participate.

---

27   "Vanguard Portfolio Allocation Models," Vanguard, https://www.vanguard.com/us/insights/saving-investing/model-portfolio-allocations.

The conferences we run, the blogs we write, and the publications we distribute all help. But it is the trading platform outlined in the previous chapter that would be the real game changer. Harnessing the power of the Internet to bring people together to do business and learn from each other is one of the best uses of our virtual connections.

So, what do you say? Are you ready to add a new investment sector to your portfolio and make it more likely that you will reach your investment goals? If so, come over to the Non-Conventional Lending Exchange. We'll walk you through everything you need to know and put you in touch with as much professional support as you need. No experience necessary.

KEY TAKEAWAYS FROM CHAPTER 9:

1. Don't let life happen to you—you should happen to life! Start taking the initiative to learn about non-conventional lending and figure out how to add it to your existing portfolio.

TAKE ACTION *NOW*

1. This plan won't act on itself. Start acting *now*.

2. Set a plan to educate yourself and invest in your first non-conventional loan or mortgage fund six months from the time you finish this book.

3. Go to our exchange platform, website, and of course, lending guide to do so.

4. Reach out to me (a.geraci@geracillp.com). How can I help you achieve your goals?

Check out these websites for more information:

Non-Conventional Lending Guide Chapter 9:
http://www.nonconlendingguide.com/chapter9

Originate Report (to network with non-conventional lenders):
http://www.originate.report

Educate yourself at a GeraciCon conference:
http://www.geracicon.com

Get on the exchange: http://www.nonconexchange.com

KEY QUESTION:

On a scale of one to ten, how likely are you going to take action on this *now*?

APPENDIX

Q: What is non-conventional lending?

A: At its core, non-conventional lending is a transaction between individuals, where one person supplies financing that another needs. While technically these loans can be used for any purpose, in reality they are almost always used for business purposes where the underlying collateral is real estate. It is this collateral that assures the lender will recoup his or her capital. (See **chapter 2: The Dawn of a New Investment Sector**)

Q: Where does the money come from?

A: The capital is supplied by investors who view this sector as a way to achieve higher-than-average, fixed-income returns while taking on relatively little risk. These investors might invest directly with the borrower, supply capital to a broker who finances non-conventional loans, or even invest with a commingled fund that invests in these private loans. (See **chapter 3: Non-Conventional Lending Explained**)

Q: What type of borrower uses non-conventional loans?

A: Typical borrowers are entrepreneurs who are responsible and creditworthy but don't fit the requirements of a standard bank. They might be self-employed or have a short employment history. Because they are often looking to flip a house, they might be carrying too much debt, even if it is short-term debt. They are often looking for short-term financing, while banks prefer longer-term mortgages. There are all sorts of scenarios, but the bottom line is the borrower is typically very capable of meeting the loan terms; they just don't meet the requirements of a bank. (See **chapter 4: The Different Flavors of Loans and Borrowers**)

Q: Why would a borrower want a private loan, as opposed to a bank loan?

A: Non-conventional loans are more flexible than a standard bank loan and thus are perfect for nonstandard situations. They can often be disbursed in a week or so, as opposed to the six to eight weeks common for bank loans. Interest rates, repayment terms, and payout schedules are all negotiable. These loans just make lots of sense for an entrepreneur who is looking for quick, short-term financing or financing with negotiable terms. (See **chapter 4: The Different Flavors of Loans and Borrowers**)

Q: What does the borrower use for collateral?

A: Technically, the borrower can use anything that the lender accepts. Realistically, real estate is the basis for non-conventional lending. Lenders hold a lien on a property that allows them to seize the property in case of default. Knowing that they have a real asset as collateral allows the lender to be more flexible in terms of borrower credit and repayment terms. (See **chapter 3: Non-Conventional Lending Explained**)

Q: How does the lender evaluate the real estate?

A: The lender performs the same due diligence that anyone seeking to purchase the property would. They look at comps, walk the property, and have the home inspected. Because the property is the collateral, the lender must be assured that if the borrower defaults, the sale of the property will cover the outstanding loan amount. Lenders tend to be conservative in their appraisals to be sure they are covered. (See **chapter 5: Becoming Part of the Non-Conventional Lending World**)

Q: What interest rate can I expect to earn as a lender?

A: The interest rate is negotiable, but in general, lenders look to earn 8 percent to 12 percent. Interest rates can take the risk into account, as well as what standard mortgages are costing. A non-conventional loan should return several percentage points over a bank loan. (See **chapter 3: Non-Conventional Lending Explained**)

Q: What is the typical length of a non-conventional loan?

A: Non-conventional loans can span any time frame agreed upon by the lender and borrower, but most tend to be shorter than bank loans. Because this is relatively expensive money, borrowers usually aim to keep the time frame to less than a year, often less than six months. (See **chapter 3: Non-Conventional Lending Explained**)

Q: What happens if the borrower defaults on the loan?

A: If the borrower defaults, the lender typically has the right to take over the property and sell it to pay off the loan. The lender normally has the contractual right to keep the entire sales price, even if it is more than the loan amount. Some lenders prefer to sell the loan as a nonperforming loan for a discount. This strategy means they lose some of their principal but don't spend additional time and money selling the property. (See **chapter 3: Non-Conventional Lending Explained**)

Q: When is the best time to make non-conventional loans?

A: Non-conventional loans are profitable in any investment and economic climate, so the best time is right now. (See **chapter 6: Investing for Today's [and Tomorrow's] Economy**)

Q: How can I get involved as a lender?

A: As a newcomer, you will probably want to start by investing through an experienced broker or by investing in a fund that finances non-conventional loans. This will allow you to get your feet wet and learn more about the sector without having to know all the details yourself. Most investors never invest directly with borrowers. They almost always use an experienced broker who has contacts with experienced accountants and lawyers, as well as qualified borrowers. (See **chapter 5: Becoming Part of the Non-Conventional Lending World**)

Q: How do I find a broker or a fund?

A: Right now, the best way is to get on the phone and begin making calls to brokers in your area. Ask if they handle non-conventional loans. Once you find a couple who say they do, ask about their experience and results. You'll want to meet face-to-face to make sure you click. You are looking for someone you can work with long-term— feeling comfortable with them is important. If you prefer a fund, you can ask local brokers about any they might run. You can also find commingled funds through a Google search. Just remember, you need to research these funds just as you would any investment. This is a great investment opportunity, but not every fund has the same success. Check out the fees and the historical returns. (See **chapter 5: Becoming Part of the Non-Conventional Lending World**)

Q: How do I learn more about non-conventional lending?

A: One of the best ways is to visit my website—www.geracilaw-firm.com—and sign up for the newsletters. You can also set up an appointment to talk to any of us about the sector and opportunities in your area.